DO I HAVE TO TAKE A PAY CUT TO WORK AT HOME?

For years Americans have been moving toward home office–based businesses. And now the self-employed are becoming increasingly successful. What kind of business can you start from your home? How do you get started? This book answers the most pressing questions you have in this exciting area.

- What are the tax advantages of working out of my own home?
- How can I get people to take me seriously?
- What kind of insurance do I need?
- How do I stay disciplined in a flexible environment?
- What is the best way to expand my business—and reinvest for greater profits?

How to Start a Successful Home Business

Money® magazine

How to Start a Successful Home Business

by Karen Cheney and Lesley Alderman

WARNER BOOKS

A Time Warner Company

A NOTE FROM THE PUBLISHER

This publication is designed to provide competent and reliable information regarding the subject matter covered. However, it is sold with the understanding that the author and publisher are not engaged in rendering legal, financial, or other professional advice. Laws and practices often vary from state to state and if legal or other expert assistance is required, the services of a professional should be sought. The author and publisher specifically disclaim any liability that is incurred from the use or application of the contents of this book.

Warner Books, Inc., 1271 Avenue of the Americas, New York, NY 10020
Visit our Web site at
http://warnerbooks.com

 A Time Warner Company

Printed in the United States of America
First Printing: November 1997
10 9 8 7 6 5 4 3 2 1

Library of Congress Cataloging-in-Publication Data

Cheney, Karen
   How to start a successful home business / Karen Cheney and Lesley
Alderman
      p. cm.
   Includes index.
   ISBN 0-446-67316-1
      1. Home–based businesses—Management. 2. New business
enterprises. I. Alderman, Lesley. II. Title.
HD62.38.C48   1997
658'.041—DC21   97-8920
                                                                CIP

Book design and text composition by L & G McRee
Cover design by Bernadette Evangelist
Cover illustration by Peter Hoey

ACKNOWLEDGMENTS

You can't start a business without the support and help of friends, family, colleagues, and other professionals. The same is true for writing a book. We couldn't have produced *How to Start a Successful Home Business* without a great deal of assistance. First, we want to thank **MONEY** Managing Editor Frank Lalli for allowing us to work on the book together and supporting us throughout the project. Many thanks, too, to **MONEY** Executive Editor Richard Eisenberg for helping the project run smoothly.

Many experts also generously gave their time and advice: Financial Planner, Lew Altfest; Alan Cohn of Sage Financial Group; Gene Fairbrother of the National Association of the Self-Employed; Carolyn Tice, executive editor of the American Home Business Association's *Home Business News*; and Beverly Williams, American Association of Home Based Businesses. In addition, we'd like to thank two superb editors and friends, Kevin Grey and Karen's husband Tom Avril.

A very special thanks to our colleague Joan Caplin, who provided indispensable reporting assistance. And, of course, we couldn't have written this book without the insights of the scores of home business entrepreneurs we interviewed. They enthusiastically shared many of their trials and triumphs. We're grateful for their candor and wish them continued success.

CONTENTS

CONTENTS

How to Start a Successful Home Business

INTRODUCTION

Is a Home Business for You?

If you're looking for a business that will generate big profits, let you work at home, and provide long-term growth, this book is for you. It will help you turn your nascent idea into a thriving enterprise. Whether you're a newly minted grad or a seasoned employee looking for a change, there are limitless possibilities for starting a business in your home.

In fact, thousands of new home businesses are started each day in mainstream fields like management consulting and public relations, as well as in emerging areas like multimedia production and personalized book publishing. And these businesses are pulling in top dollars. In an exclusive **MONEY** magazine poll conducted in 1996 by ICR Research, one out of five home entrepreneurs reported that their businesses earned between $100,000 and $500,000 in 1995. But if you hit on a great idea and develop and market it carefully, you have the potential to earn far more.

Not sure what kind of business you'd like to start? We'll show you how to draw on your skills, uncover a market niche, and hitch your efforts to one or more of the hot trends we identify. To guide you further, in Chapter 2 we profile 10 home business winners and explain what skills you need to succeed in these enterprises, as well as detail their start-up costs and income potential.

From our years of experience reporting and writing for **MONEY** magazine, the country's leading personal finance magazine, we can help you get your business on firm financial ground. We'll tell you where to find the funding to get started (Chapter 3), how to choose equipment and set up health and retirement plans (Chapter 4), and how to avoid getting snagged by tricky IRS rules (Chapter 5).

We've included many amusing and instructive stories from the real pros—the scores of successful home entrepreneurs we interviewed for this book. They'll tell you firsthand what it takes to run a business, as well as how to keep your marriage and kids happy while you're putting in 12-hour days at home. They'll also share their favorite low-cost marketing techniques and how to clinch the next customer.

While it may sound daunting, if you take it step by step, you can join the 16 million Americans who are already running businesses from their homes full time. We hope this book will both inspire you and act as your guide.

The Time Is Right

Chances are you've thought about starting your own business for years. In fact, 30% of the population is constantly thinking about going solo, according to the U.S. Small Business Administration (SBA). You may have a friend who happily traded the trappings of corporate life for the freedom, flexibility, and challenge of self-employment. An acquaintance may have launched a business at home that allows her time with the kids *and* provides for a profitable career. You may even know a recent college graduate who opted to work from home, perhaps designing Web sites for large, brand-name corporations, rather than joining the throngs of daily commuters. If you can't think of anyone who earns a living by working at home, just look around your own neighborhood and you'll likely meet such an entrepreneur. The fact is, it's easier and more practical today to run your own business from home than ever before. And the stats are on your side. Small business failures are falling, according to the SBA. In 1992 fully 15% of that year's estimated 650,000 start-ups went belly up within a year. For 1995 launches, the SBA estimates the comparable number will clock in at a mere 8%.

Start-up costs are low. Thanks to the decreasing price and rapidly increasing sophistication of technology, you don't need a secretary or even a bookkeeper to help you throw open the doors to your business. With a $5,000 investment in a basic computer, a printer, a facsimile machine, and a voice-mail system, you can make your office as efficient as a Fortune 500 company.

You can work from nearly any location. It doesn't matter if you live in a large metropolitan area like Washington, D.C., or a tiny mountain town like Ouray, Colorado; simply plug in a modem and you'll be just as connected to the world as the legions of office dwellers in midtown Manhattan. While zoning regulations may restrict you from operating certain businesses—for instance, ones that increase traffic in your neighborhood—you'll find that you can run thousands of different businesses right from your house.

Small, niche businesses are in demand. If technology has made working from home easier and less expensive, workforce trends have made it more necessary. With companies ceaselessly looking for ways to rein in expenses, annual raises have been stuck for the past few years at 2% to 3%—and that's just for those who have been able to *keep* their corporate jobs. Nearly three million people have been laid off in the past five years, according to the outplacement firm Challenger, Gray & Christmas.

But the good news is that companies are contracting out for many of the very same specialized services they slashed. For instance, when contact lens maker CooperVision eliminated Julie Kaufman's job, she turned her 10 years of market research experience into a thriving business. Now she earns six figures doing research for pharmaceutical companies. Better still, she has more time to spend with her two children and husband.

There's greater respect for home businesses. With so many educated, white-collar workers heading home to do business, there's greater acceptance of such arrangements. What's more, high-quality marketing materials you can design on your own computer will make your business look just as professional as an AT&T or a General Electric.

There Is a Home Business for Everyone

The clearest route to running your own business is to start with the skills and expertise you've developed over the years. If you're already an ace software developer, for instance, you may want to market your ability to companies looking for specialized technology.

Or it could be that during your years of corporate ladder–climbing, you noticed an entirely untapped market in your field. For instance, while selling ads for a trade magazine serving the gift industry, Millie Szerman noticed that gift manufacturers needed help with publicity. So she launched a public relations firm that helps such businesses promote their goods in print media and television.

If you're tired of working in the same field and want a bigger change, consider turning your hobby into a business. There's nothing better than getting paid to do what you enjoy most. If you love cooking, become a caterer. If reading books is your favorite pastime and you like to write, become a reviewer. Whatever product or service you're most interested in delivering, if you can find a market for it, you're in business.

Write Your Own Paycheck

Working at home makes financial sense, too. If you already have a well-equipped home office, you're halfway there. With an infusion of just a few thousand dollars for extra equipment, stationery, and professional fees, you'll be ready for business. In fact, many well-known companies were started in the family garage, basement, or on the dining room table, including Ben & Jerry's, Celestial Seasonings, and Lillian Vernon.

Low overhead. A great advantage to starting at home is that your costs will be relatively low. If you were to launch your business in a "real office" you'd have to pay hundreds of dollars (possibly even thousands) each month for rent and hefty business utility rates, as well as the cost of furniture and accessories.

No commuting costs (or hassles). You'll also save by staying close to home. You won't have to dole out cash month after month on commuting costs like gas, train fare, and parking—not to mention those hefty cell phone bills you racked up arranging your life from your car. You'll probably adopt a more casual attire, too, and won't have to spend hundreds to keep your wardrobe au courant and your clothes dry-cleaned.

Deductible expenses. You'll be able to deduct many of the expenses of your home office, including supplies you buy— everything from tape to filing cabinets—and possibly a portion of your mortgage, homeowner's insurance, and utility bills. In fact, if you decide to gussy up your house with a new coat of paint, you may even be able to deduct part of that expense, too.

You reap the profits. What's more, all the gains will be yours. If you decide to log in 12-hour days, seven days a week, and turn your company into the next Netscape, the fruits of your industrious labor will be all yours. With energy, ambition, and a great idea, the potential for your home business is boundless. Of course, starting a business in your home is no cakewalk. An alarming number of companies fail in their first few years of operation, and you could lose all the cash you socked into the business. But by starting the enterprise at home, your initial outlay will be modest, and your risk minimized.

Having It Your Way

Hands down, the biggest draw to starting a business at home is having more control over your time. Sure, you may end up working longer hours, but they will be *your* hours. And you'll be able to fit in trips to the grocery store, your kid's parent-teacher conference, and visits to see your mom in the nursing home without having to get clearance from the boss. You can create a schedule that fits in with your natural rhythms, whether that means getting up before dawn to work when your brain is liveliest and closing down at 4 P.M., or spending the mornings with your kids and clocking in your eight hours from 10 A.M. to 6 P.M. You'll be able to listen to the radio all day, take 10-minute naps when you feel groggy, eat great meals of leftovers from the night before, and weed your garden at lunchtime.

Because you are in charge you're also apt to be and *feel* more productive. You won't waste time in boring meetings (unless you call them), chitchatting around the coffee machine, or tracking down five superiors to get approval on a new procedure. You're the boss now. And you'll probably have an extra hour or two in your schedule that you would have otherwise spent in a stressful commute. According to a survey by AT&T Home Resources, 80% of home business owners say they're more productive than when they worked in a traditional office.

And you'll be able to spend more quality time with your spouse and kids. The hour you spend eating breakfast with your nine-year-old before he gets on the school bus may be reason enough to hand in your corporate ID and head home to work. Doug Shaw, a management consultant in Newtown, Pennsylvania, who opened up his home business in 1993, says those ten-minute moments when his daughter Hannah knocks on his door to tell him about a book she just read are priceless: "Who knows how many of those times I've missed over the years."

Are You Ready?

Sounds ideal, right? Big bucks and everything on your terms (finally). Well, not exactly. Soloists typically work longer hours, often find themselves longing for the camaraderie at their old workplace, and have to learn to wear many hats, from office cleaner to CEO. What's more, your only financial security is yourself, and many businesses go belly-up for lack of realistic planning.

Besides developing a top-notch business plan and a savvy marketing strategy, you'll also need an entrepreneurial spirit. In fact, after interviewing hundreds of home business owners we found there were certain characteristics that the most successful ones shared. More often than not, they had to work at developing these qualities over the years. If the following list of attributes seems daunting, take heart. We give you tips in Chapter 7 on how to develop an entrepreneur's winning mindset.

SELF-DISCIPLINE

"When there isn't somebody sitting in the room with you, it's easy to hop on the Internet and waste time," says home-based computer and actuarial consultant Christopher Maher. "You need to make sure you get your work done. Running a business at home requires a discipline that's pretty easy to find most days, but it's harder other days."

PATIENCE

"Sometimes you get clients who don't understand your business and think you can work miracles in a short period of time," says Millie Szerman, a home-based PR specialist featured on the March 1996 cover of **MONEY**.

PERSISTENCE

"I called one prospective client six times," says advertising pro Tom Wotherspoon. "You have to be persistent with leads, because you never know. I make a lot of calls. Maybe one out of 10 comes through. The worst thing you can do is say I've contacted three people and they don't want to see my portfolio. My God, that's three out of hundreds of prospects that are out there."

AN OUTGOING ATTITUDE

"The thing that's carried me through with my business is that I really enjoy meeting people and talking to them," says Loren Steen, owner of a home-based seafood brokerage. "And being outgoing helps with sales."

CREATIVITY

"Unless you're extremely well funded, money is an issue. So you have to be creative in coming up with solutions when you have limited resources," says Srinivasan Sriram, who runs a software development company from home. "Just being in the game forces you to be more creative. . . . The scope of what you can do is enormous."

COURAGE

"The first reason people fail when they start a new business is lack of money," says home-based journalist and tax consultant Joe Anthony. "The second is panic. You need to be both financially and emotionally prepared to succeed."

VERSATILITY

"I am like a one-person production company," says children's book writer Eric Arnold. "I am writer, public relations expert, and marketing whiz. It takes a lot of skills to work and do well on your own."

BUSINESS SMARTS

"What keeps your business afloat is foresight," observes New York City digital video producer Bernice Mast. "You have to know where your skills fit into the marketplace and then you have to monitor very closely how the marketplace is changing, in order to keep your business growing."

CHAPTER 1

Nailing a Six-Figure Idea

Millions of people just like you dream of starting a business. Why, then, aren't more entrepreneur wanna-bes hanging out a shingle every day? In fact, most of them would swiftly take the leap to independence but for one of two big hurdles: Either the perfect idea hasn't fallen in their laps, or they come up with possible ventures all the time but can't bring themselves to take a risk. Those in the first group think that a Netscape-level concept, poised to become Wall Street's next darling, will simply come to them in the night. In the meantime, they're stuck waiting for an epiphany. Those in the second camp, on the other hand, have a fresh business vision every other day. But they snap out of it as soon as they glance at their five-digit credit card bills and underfunded retirement plans. They can't afford to cut loose from the corporation to follow some harebrained whim!

Whether you tend to fall in the "waiting-for-a-sign" camp or the "can't-take-a-risk" one, there's a simple way to vault over these obstacles: research. Let's be real—you can't expect to wake up one morning with a perfectly honed business idea. You'll have to do a lot of digging, reading, and investigating before

11

you come up with a first-rate concept. Even once you have a business notion, you'll need to test it and fine-tune it before you go solo. In fact, you're right about not cutting loose from the corporation. To eliminate some of the risks of going into business, you'll have to research your idea and test it in the marketplace—and that requires both time and money. In other words, hang on to your nine-to-five job and use weekends, the wee hours, and workplace downtime to do some preliminary research.

In this chapter, we'll help you get started by showing you how to:

- Turn your skills into your company
- Spot under-served market niches
- Research trends—and tap the seven major ones we outline
- Test your idea before you go solo
- Determine if a franchise is best for you
- Check out zoning restrictions
- Avoid get-rich-quick scams
- Protect your idea

Leverage Your Skills into a Business

As you begin trolling for business ideas, the most logical place to start is in your own field. Whether you're an accountant, a secretary, or a nurse's aide, you can turn your salaried job into a home enterprise. Take, for instance, computer whiz Jay Horowitz. He worked for half a dozen years as a programmer and systems analyst for such large corporations as Merrill Lynch and Citibank. "All along," he says, "I had a sideline business of clients I would see after hours." Horowitz was smart. Before going solo full time, he built up a substantial network of customers. Now he develops software and provides computer support primarily to financial services firms and brokerages. Although his work is similar to what he did in his salaried job, he's far happier setting his own hours and watching his profits go entirely to his own bottom line.

If you prefer to venture out on a slightly different course, begin by seeking out new opportunities within your field. That way you'll have the advantage of operating in an area you already know well. Millie Szerman, for example, used to sell ad space for *Gifts & Decorative Accessories* trade magazine. While working for the magazine, she began to notice that many small gift manufacturers needed help generating publicity for their products. "I'd never done public relations before," she admits, "but I have the gift of gab, a flair for language, and a very solid background in sales and marketing." These skills, combined with a strong familiarity with the gift industry, helped her rev up her PR business in no time.

TAKE A SELF-INVENTORY

It may sound like a goofy exercise you did as a senior in high school, but by writing down your strengths and weaknesses, you'll stay focused on finding the business that suits you best. So take out a piece of paper, scribble down the following subheads, and make a list under each one:

Skills. Think of all the things you've learned how to do over the years, such as bookkeeping, programming computers, or typing.

Talents. What do you do well innately? Are you an ace decorator, puzzle solver, or organizer?

Hobbies. Don't forget to list the activities you love so much that you carve out time for them no matter how busy you are. One of them may have business potential.

Industries I know. You may have worked in sales, for instance, in a number of different industries. Even if you've stayed in the same field, you've probably had some contact with other areas. For instance, journalists typically know something about public relations, because they often work with PR experts.

Weaknesses. It's just as important to take note of what you *don't* do well. While you may be able to learn new skills, you should start a business that capitalizes on your strengths.

Dislikes. Just because you're good at something doesn't mean that you enjoy it. Of course, keep in mind that with any business, you'll have to do a number of tasks you don't relish—whether that's keeping careful records of expenses or finding new customers.

Next, on a second sheet of paper, jot down as many business ideas you can think of that require the smarts, talents, and experience you just listed. You'll be surprised by the number of possible ventures you could start on your own.

Okay, so what if you want to pursue a business in a field that's entirely new to you? As long as you're willing to learn new skills, there's no reason you can't. But before you take off on an around-the-world search for a novel idea, don't overlook a possible moneymaking opportunity right under your nose: your hobbies and favorite pastimes. If you've always enjoyed throwing parties, consider becoming an event coordinator. Does following the stock market's gyrations and investing give you a thrill? Become a financial planner (a hot business we discuss in Chapter 2). If collecting art is your passion, start a business advising corporations and individuals on the purchase of art. Bottom line: Whether your skills lead you to a new field or not, you should pursue a business you enjoy. "Sometimes we sit here and laugh, because we're doing something we love and people are paying us money for it," says Elizabeth Cyran, who started a photography business with her husband, Franklyn.

FOR MORE INFORMATION

• The classic career guide *What Color Is Your Parachute?* ($16.95; Ten Speed Press) will help you hone in on your strengths and interests.

• *Finding Your Perfect Work* by Paul and Sarah Edwards ($16.95; Jeremy P. Tarcher/Putnam) can bring focus to your search by helping you determine your priorities.

Find a Market Niche

While you're hunting for ideas, keep in mind that ideally you want to hit on a business that will serve a market niche. Most entrepreneurs, you'll find, launch familiar concepts like child day care, accounting, or cleaning services. As long as the competition in their area isn't fierce, they can usually earn a decent living. But to make serious money in a home business, you need to uncover a place in the market that's not being served by anything out there. Just consider some of today's successful businesses that started in a basement, on a dining room table, or in a spare room. The accounting software company Intuit, for instance, came about when Scott Cook and Tom Proulx created a program called Quicken for keeping track of personal finances. Quicken is so easy to use that it has been able to reach a massive, formerly under-served market: the average person. Other homegrown businesses have had similar success. Ben & Jerry's tapped the ex-hippie, boomer generation with its gourmet ice cream, and Lillian Vernon offered convenient, mail-order gift shopping.

How can you find a niche? Like Millie Szerman, who noticed that there was a dearth of public relations professionals in the gift industry, you have to keep your eyes open to every possibility. Here are some tips:

• **Solve Problems.** Every time a friend or relative moans about the poor service they got at a store or how they can't find the exact product they need, they're not just whining. They're giving you business ideas—free of charge. For instance, how often have you heard someone groan about buying a used car that started to sputter and stall a week later? Voilà! Enter the used-car superstores that offer engine and body checkups and may even provide a warranty.

What bothers you most about the products and services you use every day? For Carmela Cantisani the answer was that she couldn't find real French salad dressing in the United States. Cantisani, an Italian-American, studied in Paris, where she became accustomed to fine French dressing made with rich olive oil and fresh herbs. "I was always turned off by the dressings here, and I felt that they were misleading," says Cantisani. "French dressing in the United States doesn't begin to resemble an authentic French vinaigrette." After testing her idea by selling samples in local stores, Cantisani determined that she had found a market niche. "Each year, we sell more and more," she says. "Now we have a nice line of three different products."

• **Fill a Wish.** While you're listening to people complain about what they don't have, pay attention to what they wish they *did* have. "A lot of women have said, 'I wish I had a wife to run errands for me,'" says Arnold Brown, chairman of Weiner, Edrich, Brown, Inc., a consulting firm specializing in trend analysis. "Well, now you see concierge services in every office building to run your errands, make appointments, even buy your holiday gifts."

• **Meet a Special Need.** Take a look at groups of people with needs that are hard to fill such as the disabled and the elderly. Are there any products or services you could offer them that would make their lives fuller or easier? For instance, you might start a limousine service to take elderly people to evening events at the theater or opera. If you enjoy cooking, you might prepare meals and start a delivery service. Or you could look into possibilities in home health care for people with chronic conditions.

• **Interpret New Regulations.** Whenever the government changes the tax code or passes a new piece of legislation on health care, a new market niche is born. After all, businesses and individuals need consultants to explain how those changes may affect them. There may be new tax deductions they can take advantage of, or they may need to learn how to comply with a new law. Some regulations may even create openings for new products like medical savings accounts or new pension plans.

CHECK YOUR LOCAL LAWS

Before you get too revved up about your business idea, call your local zoning board, community development office, or planning department to find out if there are any restrictions on home businesses in your area. Traditionally, communities have allowed professionals like doctors and lawyers to work out of a residence, but now many are broadening the range of businesses they consider appropriate home occupations. Nevertheless, most planning boards place some restrictions even on permissible businesses, according to the American Planning Association. For instance, zoning laws may dictate the amount of parking and traffic allowed, the number of nonresident employees, the size and shape of business signs, the percentage of a residence that can be used for business, where equipment is stored, and hours of operation. Len and Carolyn Vertin of Santa Cruz, California, for example, had no trouble getting a permit for their bookkeeping business. But they have to comply with strict rules limiting them to no more than one employee and only six client visits a day.

If the type of business you want to run isn't specifically mentioned in the regulations, ask the zoning board for a variance—an exemption from some portion of the zoning law. Typically, this involves filling out forms detailing the business activities you plan to carry on at home. The board may then notify your neighbors by mail, or it may choose to call a public hearing. If no one objects to your plan and the board approves it, you're in business. If you have trouble getting a variance, consider lobbying to change the law. You'll need to enlist the support of

---

your neighbors and other home entrepreneurs and appeal to city council members. While many home enterprises operate illegally, you don't want to run the risk of being put out of business and possibly fined for violating the law.

Keep in mind that to find a market niche, you don't need to come up with an entirely original product or service. You can simply take an old product and position it differently via the following ways:

• **Cost.** By pricing the same product your competitors offer at a lower price, you might reach a wider market. Conversely, you might do better appealing to a select audience by making your product more expensive. Of course, you'll have to enhance your offerings to make them worth a higher price.

• **Service.** Adding more or better service is a sure way to stand out from competitors. For instance, if three people in town offer child day-care services, you might offer the same service but also agree to pick up and drop off your charges.

• **Quality.** You can also take a familiar product and improve its quality. Quicken, for example, was not the first financial planning tool available. However, it became the number-one-selling software because it's easier to use than the others and has first-rate graphics.

Tap Major Trends

As if finding a market niche weren't enough, you need to fill it with a product or service that you're sure will be in demand for years. That's where spotting trends comes into play. The most successful entrepreneurs possess an amazing knack for predicting subtle shifts in the economy. They foresee more people working at home in the future, for instance, so they create home-office supply stores like Staples. They sense that people will become increasingly concerned about medical care, so they start services to provide medical information that doctors today have less time to dispense. They anticipate more companies doing business overseas, so they set up global business consulting firms.

To investigate the trends in your field, start attending trade shows and perusing specialized business magazines. Because these publications cover just one industry, they're usually more on top of trends than a general-interest magazine. Of course, you should still read business magazines like *Fortune*, *Your Company*, and *Business Week*. "It's also a good idea to subscribe to at least one publication that infuriates you," says Brown of the trend-tracking firm Weiner, Edrich, Brown, Inc. The reason, he says: "You need to start taking in information that you would otherwise reject."

And don't neglect to spend a few hours each week canvassing the World Wide Web. On-line research offers a bonanza of information—most of which is totally free. For a directory of company Web addresses, try Open Market's Commercial Sites Index (http://www.directory.net), where you'll find tens of thousands of company listings, and BizWeb (http://www.bizweb.com), which also serves as an electronic Yellow Pages. If you're interested in searching a specific topic—whether it's baseball cards, Barbie, or Bombay—try a search engine like Yahoo (http://www.yahoo.com) or AltaVista (http://www.altavista.digital.com). Both will ask you to enter key words and then will search their databases for appropriate Web sites.

To help you get started tracking trends, we've outlined seven major growth areas that are pushing the economy into the twenty-first century:

• **Business-to-business services.** Ever since the early '90s, downsized companies have saved money by outsourcing functions like sales, employee benefits administration, and computer network maintenance. This has created rich opportunities for both consultants and temporary workers. In fact, we're likely to see a boom in personnel supply services over the next decade, according to the Bureau of Labor Statistics (for more information on temp services that can be run out of your home, see Chapter 2).

CHOOSING THE RIGHT FRANCHISE

Visit any strip mall in the country, and you won't be surprised to hear that franchising companies and their franchisees account for 41% of U.S. retail sales. In fact, every eight minutes a new franchise outlet pops up in a mall, an airport, a small rural town, or a big city. Since starting a new business can be risky, it's no wonder many entrepreneurs end up deciding to buy a franchise from a company with a proven track record. What's more, an increasing number of franchisors offer home-based formats. Mark Siebert, president of the consulting company Francorp, says that as many as 400 franchise companies can be run from the comfort of your spare bedroom. That's a fivefold increase in just a few years' time.

Roughly 23% of home-based franchises are in residential and commercial cleaning, but you'll also find franchises in home inspection services, pest control, home restoration, computer training and consulting, Web page consulting, tax services, payroll services, and tutoring. In fact, good franchises take advantage of the trends that we outline in this chapter. For instance, Crestcom International offers management training seminars to small companies on such topics as recruiting, conflict resolution, delegating work, and dealing with change. The company's training program uses a combination of live and video-based instruction, which franchisees have the rights to use. Bob Sanner said that he became a Crestcom franchisee in 1992 because the quality of the videos was unmatchable. "It would have taken millions of dollars for me to create the high-quality training materials Crestcom offers," says Sanner. After paying distribution fees, royalties, and costs for the materials, he pockets about half of his $10,000 average sale.

But is buying a franchise the right move for you? When you purchase a franchise, you pay the franchisor for the right to use its trademark, name, products, and business format in exchange for an initial fee and ongoing royalties. You get the benefit of buying a business that has already been tested and may have name recognition. In addition, you may receive training and support, as well as advertising and economies of scale if the franchisor sells you products in bulk. But on the downside, you have to pay steep fees—generally $10,000 to $100,000 for a home-based franchise—and you give up control. Franchisors typically set standards and can dictate to you how you have to run your business. They may even have the right to terminate your agreement if they don't feel that you're meeting expectations.

If you still think that franchising is the best way for you to get into business, make sure you sign on with a franchisor that has a bright future serving a niche in your market. To find out how much support you'll receive as a franchisee, get on the phone. "The best thing to do is to call every one of the franchisees— up to a reasonable amount," says Siebert. "Ask tough questions. Are they satisfied with performance?" You can get numbers of franchisees from the Uniform Franchise Offering Circular, a disclosure document the franchisor must give you. The UFOC also lists the costs for such items as the one-time franchising fee, ongoing royalties, and estimates for necessary equipment, training, and inventory. For more information on franchising, contact the International Franchise Association (202-628-8000). The IFA runs a trade show every spring in Washington, D.C., featuring more than 300 different companies (call 800-829-3976 if you're interested in attending).

Technology gurus, product marketers, videoconference planners, and individuals with an expertise in government and environmental regulations are in particular demand. Rather than simply advising companies, consultants are spending more time working on long-term projects, according to the Institute of Management Consultants. Companies also want more customized services, which small home businesses are better suited to deliver. "Big consulting firms tend to standardize their services," says Larry Dressler, a home-based consultant specializing in organizational development. "The companies that buy from us believe that they're unique, and they want special services." With more companies pulling in squads of experts to work intensely on short-term projects and then disband, Dressler's company, Creative Team Solutions, fills an important niche by helping build these project-oriented groups into successful teams.

• **Increased education needs.** "Education is still designed for the industrial age," says Jennifer Jarratt of the trend research firm Coates & Jarratt. But in the future, she predicts, people will look at education as an ongoing process. For one, technology has been advancing so swiftly that people have to seek further training to keep up with it. The International Franchise Association reports that one of the biggest growth areas in franchising is in children's education, particularly computer training (for more info on franchising, see the box on page 20). What's more, American workers are beginning to career-hop from industry to industry, requiring them to pick up vastly different skills along the way. This opens up many opportunities for career counselors, educators, and training consultants.

• **Global trade.** While only 11% of small businesses exported products in the early '90s, by 2005, about one-third of businesses will be shipping their goods and services overseas, according to the Small Business Administration. As a result, there will be a heightened need for experts on foreign market conditions and pros who advise businesses on setting up branches abroad. "There's a market there to be harnessed—in the area of helping with regulations, understanding local business cultures, freight and logistics, staff relocation and training," says Pete Collins, director of entrepreneurial advisory services at Coopers & Lybrand. "There are lots of opportunities to ride the globalization wave." In Chapter 2, we'll profile another savvy business that takes advantage of this trend: export agents who act as liaisons between buyers and sellers in the United States and abroad.

• **Health-care services.** The health services industry accounts for a hefty 9% of the country's total employment. In fact, seven of the 20 fastest-growing occupations, according to the BLS, are in health care, which is expected to grow twice as fast as the rest of the economy. The biggest winner within health services: home health care. The reason is clear. On the one hand, cost containment pressures are forcing hospitals around the country to close. On the other hand, people are living longer with more chronic illness. As a result, care is shifting from medical institutions to private homes. Realizing that need prompted Julie Huckaby, Karen Bairaktaris, and Pat Limbaugh to launch Omni Home Medical of Chattanooga. Their firm—born in a business incubator—contracts nurses to administer intravenous drugs to homebound patients.

Another explosive area is medical records. Despite the fact that hospitals are shutting their doors, the industry needs technicians to keep records for an increasing number of medical tests, treatments, and procedures that, according to the BLS, will undergo greater scrutiny by health insurers, courts, and consumers. Hospitals, physicians, and mental-health centers will also contract out billing services to home entrepreneurs like Robert O'Kelly, who started a medical claims processing business in Las Vegas.

• **Marketplace diversity.** Between 1992 and 2005, 14.9 million women are expected to enter the workforce, compared to 12.4 million men. We'll also see an increasing number of minority workers, especially Hispanics and Asians. The number of Hispanic workers will expand by 64%—making up more than a quarter of the new additions to the workforce, according to the Bureau of the Census. The number of Asian workers will soar by 81%—the fastest growth rate of all minorities. And blacks will add 14% to the workforce.

Along with greater marketplace and workforce diversity come opportunities for women and minority specialists in training, marketing, and creating products and services that these groups will enjoy. Marie Racioppi, for instance, has a home business teaching global companies like AT&T how to market to women, minorities, and other under-served customers. A former systems analyst for Prudential Insurance, Racioppi was introduced to the training field when she teamed with Katherine Kish to start a statewide entrepreneurial training program offered by the New Jersey Association of Women Business Owners. "We enjoyed the program so much we thought there had to be a business in there somewhere," she says.

• **Personal services.** With people feeling constantly pressed for time, businesses that save customers even as little as an hour a week are sure to be a success. "For instance, the financial markets are becoming more complex, and most people don't have the time to figure out what's happening and handle their finances themselves," says Jarratt. To help them, financial planners—many of whom work from home—develop personal financial plans (a business we discuss further in Chapter 2). In the post-industrial age, consumers will continue to demand more customized products and services, says Jarratt. Witness the growth in personal fitness trainers, private tutors, personal career counselors, and personal chefs who come to your home one day a week to prepare meals according to your specific dietary needs. We even hire others to do our gift shopping for us. For instance, Personal Shopper International advertises its business on the World Wide Web for Americans living abroad. You simply send the service a list of the products you want, and it will send you pricing and availability quotes before buying and sending the merchandise to you.

• **Technology.** Advances in science and technology will create business opportunities on many levels. For instance, you could start a business by filling an old need with new technology. "Let's say a federal lab has developed a new composite metal. You may be able to use this product to create a baseball bat that's easier to swing," says Collins. "All it takes is someone with a great deal of imagination to come up with a commercial application for technological and scientific breakthroughs."

Meanwhile, marketing pros with a flair for selling new technology should be inundated with work. Universities with large research-and-development facilities are full of scientists and technical people looking for individuals with marketing experience to sell their inventions, says Collins. And of course, as we mentioned under the heading "Business-to-business Services," companies need technology consultants to help them keep up to speed. In fact, tech experts already comprise 45% of membership in the Institute of Management Consultants.

If you're smart, you'll follow the example of Les and Barbara Kalmus. They hitched their business to two runaway trends—the demand for both technical expertise and temporary workers—and launched CyberStaff America. A temporary-services firm, CyberStaff places highly trained computer-systems pros on short-term projects at Fortune 500 companies. Business grew so quickly that within six months, the Kalmuses were forced to move from their New York City apartment to an office location.

FOR MORE INFORMATION

Besides the Web sites already mentioned above, check out these government databases:

• The Bureau of Labor Statistics (http://stats.bls.gov) publishes many reports containing such useful information as the factors influencing consumer spending and where job growth will be. For instance, a study called "Employment Outlook: 1994–2005 Job Quality and Other Aspects of Projected Employment Growth" claims that there will be 17.7 million new jobs created by 2005. A phenomenal 70% of those jobs will be in the service sector.

• U.S. Census Bureau (http://www.census.gov) offers a wealth of demographic information, such as the fastest-growing cities and states.

• Run by the syndicated columnist Rhonda Abrams, Idea Cafe (http://www.ideacafe.com) holds periodic conferences with special guests like "Dilbert" creator Scott Adams. You can pick up ideas and share your own in the "CyberSchmooz" café too.

HOW TO IDENTIFY A SHAM BUSINESS

You've seen the ads in newspapers and magazines: MAKE MILLIONS THROUGH MAIL ORDER, EARN $1,500 A WEEK STUFFING ENVELOPES, BUY OUR CRAFT KIT AND STRIKE GOLD. We don't expect you to get suckered by such obvious scams. But keep a wary eye out for some of the more sophisticated ploys:

Seminars. Many swindlers hold seminars where they trot out supposed entrepreneurs who tell glowing success stories. How do you know if the gig is a hoax? Easy. If the host tells you that the products you'll be selling are only available for a limited time, get out fast. You should never feel pressured to buy into a business.

900 numbers. Don't trust ads urging you to call a 900 number for information on home businesses. Placing a call will cost you from $10 to $18, and it will probably fail to lead to moneymaking ventures.

Superlow franchise fees. Be wary if a franchisor charges initial fees of only $495. The reason: The Federal Trade Commission requires franchises with fees of $500 or more to file disclosure documents, including the franchisor's background and names, and the addresses and phone numbers of other franchisees.

Recently the FTC has cracked down on a range of fraudulent home-based schemes—from travel agencies to medical claims billing businesses. To make sure you don't become a victim, check with your local consumer protection agency, Better Business Bureau, and the state attorney general's office to see if they have received any complaints about the company. Even more important, read your contract carefully before you sign it, warns the FTC. The salesperson may make all sorts of claims that aren't in the contract, but it's what's in the contract that counts.

Test Your Idea

Okay, so you've got a business idea that holds more promise than the Internet. Time to unveil it to the world, right? Not so fast. Before ramping up production, you need to be certain that there's a ready group of buyers for your goods or services. In other words, you need to conduct market research.

Essentially, in researching your idea, you should answer two essential questions: *Will it sell?* and *Who will buy it?* First, you must gauge the amount of demand there will be for your product or service. Next, to position your product well in terms of design, special features, price, distribution methods, and advertising, you must learn as much as you can about your potential customers—also known as your "prospects."

ANALYZE YOUR COMPETITION

Begin by checking out possible competitors. For instance, let's say you want to go into business as a personal chef. If you find that your area is glutted with personal chefs, you may have to reconsider your idea entirely. On the other hand, after doing further research, you may discover that your competitors serve only high-income households on a full-time basis. By offering to visit a customer's home one day a week and cook and freeze three to five meals, you may be able to reach the many dual-income couples who are too busy to prepare their own food but can't afford a full-time cook. So the presence of competition doesn't necessarily mean that you're out of luck. You may very well be able to position your company in a different way.

To find out what your competitors are up to, start with two of the most basic tools: the Yellow Pages and a telephone. In one simple call, you can obtain your competitor's current pricing and product information. Ask the company to send its marketing materials and brochures, too, which will give you more insight into the direction it's taking. If you think that your target audience will extend beyond your local area, your library may have a national telephone directory on CD-ROM. And, of course, don't neglect to spend time on-line. Thousands of businesses have Web sites with even more information on upcoming products and services. Go back to some of the same directories and search engines we mention under the section on trends, and look for specific Web sites.

Next, analyze where your competitors are placing advertisements. Take note if they are running repeat ads (a good sign that sales are being made), and try to discern whom they are targeting. Check with their suppliers too. They'll know what's selling well and what isn't. Finally, start attending trade and professional meetings in the industry or market you hope to serve. By networking, you'll gain valuable contacts—and you'll learn more about your potential customers and what their needs and wants are.

STUDY YOUR CUSTOMER

The fact is you'll want to know everything you can about your potential client—from eye color to shoe size. Okay, we might be exaggerating slightly, but take some time to write down everything you think you know about your typical customer now: age, sex, race, marital status, spending habits, etc. If you plan to sell to businesses, define the type of company you *think* would become a client. Is it a large, product-driven firm? To whom does it sell its goods or services? What are the primary challenges in its industry?

Focus groups. Once you've put together a sketchy profile of your potential customer or "prospect," consider holding a focus group—a type of brainstorming session in which people who might use your product or service discuss its pros and

PROTECTING YOUR IDEA

Your business idea is an asset—just like your car, your house, or your savings account. In the legal community, it's known as "intellectual property," and you may want to protect it from unauthorized use just as you would insure your house or car. After all, if you've spent years designing a new product like a software program, a safer car seat, or a low-calorie candy, you'll want a patent to keep pirates from stealing your hard work. Similarly, if you've created a slogan or logo that helps sell your new gizmo, you'll need a trademark to prevent your competitors from mimicking your look. Here's how to protect your idea:

Patents. The government grants patents to inventors to shield their innovation from unauthorized use. A utility patent is granted to anyone who comes up with a new or improved process, machine, or other product, and it lasts for 20 years. A design patent, which has a life of just 14 years, may be granted to anyone who invents a new, original, and ornamental design for an article of manufacture. Finally, there's a separate 20-year patent for the discovery or creation of a new plant. For a small company with less than 500 employees, basic filing fees for a patent are $385. Don't expect to secure one right away, however. It takes the government an average of 20 months to make sure that no one else came up with the idea before you.

Trademarks. To protect a word, logo, slogan, color or even a sound, you must seek a trademark. Basic filing fees are $245 for small enterprises. But unlike patents, trademarks can be renewed indefinitely every 10 years.

Copyrights. The Library of Congress registers copyrights on books, essays, articles, music, and works of art. A copyright lasts for the life of the author plus 50 years. Beatles recordings and *Gone with the Wind*, for example, enjoy copyright protection.

For More Information

• For the free booklets *Basic Facts about Registering a Trademark* and *Basic Facts about Patents*, write to the U.S. Patent and Trademark Office, Department of Commerce, Washington, D.C., 20231; or call 800-PTO-9199.

• The American Intellectual Property Law Association also offers an excellent booklet called *How to Protect and Benefit from Your Ideas*, along with a half-hour consultation with a member lawyer for just $10 (American Intellectual Property Law Association; 2001 Jefferson Davis Hwy., Suite 203; Arlington, Va. 22202-3694).

cons. You can hire a professional to conduct a focus group for you, or you can simply convene a group of people yourself. But make sure that you invite only those folks who fit the profile you outlined. If people in the group aren't prospects, it doesn't matter what they have to say about your product. You wouldn't want animal rights activists, for instance, to debate the pros and cons of your new fur-lined ski pants, would you?

By listening to the concerns and interests raised during the focus group, you may gain valuable insights. But you must conduct the session with specific goals in mind. It's useful to develop an outline of topics you want to cover, and you should ask the group specific questions. Would they buy your product or service? If so, how frequently? What would they pay? Listen for any indication of unique features that, if offered, would provide an advantage over the competition.

Surveys. Once you have a fairly clear picture of your customer, consider casting your net wider by conducting a survey. You can survey people by telephone or mail. If your target audience is your local area, call one out of every 10 or so names in your phone book. However, you may have a more specific customer in mind. For instance, if you've created a new type of rock-climbing gear, you should survey subscribers of climbing or outdoor magazines. You can find companies specializing in mailing lists in the Yellow Pages. For national lists, go to the library and look up a book called the *Direct Marketing Marketplace* or order a copy from the Direct Marketing Association (Direct Marketing Association, Book Distribution Center, P.O. Box 391, Annapolis Junction, MD 20701). Most lists cost from $40 to $100 for 1,000 names. "It's a good idea to buy a small quantity of names and test the list to see what kind of response you get," says Aimee Stern, editor of the newsletter *Marketing Report*.

MAKE A TRIAL RUN

If you have a service-oriented business, start taking a few clients whom you can see while you're still employed. Make sure you ask for feedback on your services. Are there things you could do better? Would the client ask for your services again? If you plan to launch a product-driven business, you should manufacture a small number of samples to send to potential customers. Find out what they liked and didn't like about the product and whether or not they would order more. You may also opt to place samples in one or two stores on a consignment basis and track how long it takes them to sell. For instance, when Cantisani started her salad dressing business, she produced an initial case of 24 bottles, placing them in local gourmet food stores. The bottles sold within weeks, and she knew she was in business.

CHAPTER 2

Ten
Home Business
Winners

These days you can turn most any skill into a home-based business—from making pottery to sell at craft fairs to designing Web sites for multinational corporations. There are literally thousands of businesses you can run right from your basement or spare room. Of course, not every home enterprise offers top income potential or opportunity for growth. Obviously, you're not likely to bring in the same money with a dog-walking service as you would with a financial planning practice.

As we explain in Chapter 1, to earn serious money, you have to find a market niche and take advantage of a growing trend. We researched hundreds of businesses and selected 10 that exemplify this strategy. In this chapter, we provide profiles of our top 10 to give you a better understanding of what comprises a winning business idea. You'll learn, for instance, how the businesses we chose take advantage of strong economic currents like the increasing demand for personal services, technological expertise, and continued training. What's more, you'll see that they don't necessarily require a huge cash infusion. A computer, a telephone, a fax machine, and a lot of ambition are typically all you need to get started. One of our 10 winners may be perfect for you. Or they may inspire you to develop a home-run idea of your own.

Employee Trainer

If you have a passion for teaching and expertise in a hot field, you may find your niche as an employee trainer. Companies turn to trainers to keep their troops up to speed on such topics as new government regulations, improved methods of selling, better procedures for handling customer relations, and smart ways to take advantage of technology. In an era of downsizing, employee trainers are in especially strong demand to act as coaches to remaining workers. They teach them how to pick up the slack and take on new responsibilities.

It's little wonder, then, that 65% of employers offer more training to their employees today than they did just three years ago, according to a survey by the American Society for Training and Development (ASTD). Even better, outside specialists end up with nearly a third of the more than $55 billion that companies spend each year teaching their employees new skills.

Hot spots: Team building, leadership training for management, career development, and technical training.

SKILLS YOU NEED

Number one, you're a teacher. That means you need top-notch speaking and presentation skills. David Spivey, an employee trainer specializing in organizational development, says that good trainers are adept at getting people involved in discussions and learning activities.

While you don't need a business degree, a nuts-and-bolts understanding of how companies operate is essential. You'll also need strong research and writing skills to analyze your clients' strengths and weaknesses. Finally, warns Spivey, "Don't be a universal trainer." It's far better to focus on one area of expertise, such as diversity training or team building.

WORK-LIFE SNAPSHOT

Most trainers offer on-site courses during business hours. However, management sometimes prefers weekend workshops, which may be administered at an off-site retreat. Some projects take months, while others last no more than a half day. Expect to put in megahours of prep time, too, since you'll probably have to tailor your program to meet a particular company's needs. What's more, you may have to provide written evaluations at the end of a project. Finally, count on logging lots of miles—unless you live near a large city and can keep busy with clients in your local area.

SPECIAL COSTS

Besides basic home office equipment, you'll have to invest in training materials—either developing your own or buying supplies from other training sources. Home-based human services trainer Lois Rood, for instance, created videos, audio tapes, and manuals for her work with hospitals, mental-health facilities, and correctional institutions in the field of developmental disabilities. As a sideline business, she sells her training kits for $250 to $400 to other trainers.

INCOME POTENTIAL

The average income ranges from $50,000 to $75,000, but the upside potential is $100,000 to $200,000 for real go-getters. Most trainers base their fees on an hourly rate or are paid by the project. A typical half-day session, for instance, garners roughly $1,500.

FOR MORE INFORMATION

• **American Society for Training and Development**, with 60,000 members, offers conferences, publications, courses, seminars, training materials on a variety of subjects and customized searches for information. National membership costs $150 a year, and local chapter memberships—a good opportunity to network—run $15 to $18 a year (800-NATASTD).

• *The Wall Street Journal* and business magazines like *Fortune* will help keep you up to date on general corporate trends.

• For training materials, cassettes, and software, call **Carlson Learning Company** for a complete brochure (612-540-5122).

• For information specific to management training, contact the **American Management Association** (800-262-9699).

Export Agent

It doesn't take an Einstein to figure out why this business is hopping. Technology is making international communication easier and the manufacture and transport of goods more efficient. What's more, the opening of Eastern Europe, the rapid economic growth of Southeast Asia, and the development of Latin America promise a world of opportunity for ambitious entrepreneurs. In fact, export sales, currently around $700 billion a year, should surge to more than $1 trillion by 2005, according to the Small Business Administration.

But businesses looking to expand abroad face numerous questions. Most important, they may not know where to begin to look for buyers of their goods or services. That's where export agents come into play. These pros locate foreign buyers for American products, or they help foreign businesses find buyers in the United States. Either way, they act as a go-between and help negotiate a price so that a sale can take place.

Hot spots: You'll find the most opportunity in developing countries, where there's strong demand for high-tech goods, machinery parts for airplanes and cars, and medical supplies. For instance, Heidi Sell helps U.S. distributors of medical products find buyers in countries as far away as Pakistan. Her narrow specialty: selling cryogenic containers for blood and organ shipments. "U.S. medical equipment is considered the best in the world," says Sell, who finds buyers by looking for their ads on the Internet.

SKILLS YOU NEED

Making contacts and looking for customers abroad takes more than sharp sales skills. The more aggressive, persistent, and resourceful you are, the better your chances of thriving as an export agent. To make things easier, most agents specialize in a particular industry or country. For instance, let's say your expertise is finding buyers in Mexico. If a company thinks that there's a market for its goods south of the border, it will contact you to help it find a buyer.

You'll be more successful as an export agent if you have some understanding of customs, overseas shipping, and international banking. For educational resources, see our list below.

WORK-LIFE SNAPSHOT

Export agents have the freedom to operate anywhere they want. However, you may get more business if you live in a so-called gateway location like Florida, New York, or California. It also helps to make occasional international trips to meet buyers face to face—both to strengthen your business relationships and gain referrals. You'll also need to travel to trade shows in the United States and abroad to scout for potential customers. Although most communication with foreign buyers is by fax and E-mail, you may have to field calls at odd hours of the night.

SPECIAL COSTS

A flush bank account (minimum $25,000). Why so much cash? Occasionally you might have to take possession of the goods in transit. In other words, you may have to pay the American seller for the goods you eventually sell to a buyer in Mexico.

INCOME POTENTIAL

If you take possession of the products, you can sell them at a markup. Otherwise, you'll merely act as a mediator and earn a commission. Average income is a generous $75,000. Those at the top ring in up to $250,000 a year.

FOR MORE INFORMATION

• **The Small Business Exporters Association** is an advocacy group for small businesses. It provides contacts, support groups, resources, and information ($395, annual membership; 703-642-2490).

• Check out the **NetSource Trade Center** (http://www.netsource-asia.com/trade.htm) for a world of information, including training sites, government regulations, and multiple listings of exporters looking for agents.

• **Export USA** (http://www.exportusa.com) is the home page of John Jagoe, an export agent who wrote the widely used guide *Export Sales & Marketing Manual* (800-876-0624).

• **Trade Compass** provides trade leads, shipping schedules, country commercial guides, as well as a "chat facility" for sending real-time messages to your trading partners in a public or private form (http://www.tradecompass.com).

• **Columbia Cascade** offers two excellent software programs: *Judging Your Export Readiness* ($69.95), which helps you define whether or not a product is exportable, and *Export Expert: The Complete Guide to the Global Trade Process* ($169.95). For orders, call 800-268-4332.

Financial Planner

The daunting array of investment choices on the market—including 9,000-plus mutual funds and dozens of arcane life insurance plans—can overwhelm the average consumer. And rightly so. Enter the financial planner, a knowledgeable pro who can help individuals cut through the morass and provide personalized investing and saving advice. Planners work with clients either on a one-time basis to develop a budget, or to provide ongoing services such as portfolio management and tax planning.

The profession is growing by leaps and bounds. The number of planners with the certified financial planner (CFP) designation surged 50% between 1990 and 1995. But increased competition isn't putting a damper on business. According to the 1996 CFP Survey in Financial Planning, 86% of CFPs say they expect their client base to increase over the next five years. Nearly one-third say the increase will be "substantial." D. J. Shah, a planner in Weston, Massachusetts, has worked solo for 15 years. His business is so brisk he is considering opening a branch office in Salt Lake City, so he can indulge his passion for skiing while building up a new client pool.

Hot spots: As baby boomers become increasingly concerned about their long-term financial security, demand for retirement planning will surge.

SKILLS YOU NEED

You don't need a specific degree to call yourself a financial planner. However, the CFP designation adds credibility and, according to insiders, can boost your earnings significantly. To receive the CFP credential you must take a 10-hour exam that covers taxes, employee benefits, retirement planning, investment management, and insurance. The exam is offered by the CFP Board (see below). In addition to credentials, you need business experience, a passion for personal finance and an interest in helping people.

WORK-LIFE SNAPSHOT

Shah's glamorous, jet-set lifestyle may sound tempting, but stay grounded: planners need to meet face to face with clients on a regular basis. That's not to say your business hours must be nine to five. Jeff Mehler, for instance, moonlights as a CFP and sees his clients on evenings and weekends.

SPECIAL COSTS

Start with a word-processing program and a spreadsheet like Excel. But soon you'll want to add a financial package like Quicken and a tax program for more in-depth analysis. Planners also subscribe to stock and mutual-fund reports like Morningstar and ValueLine. Total start-up tab: $2,000 to $3,000. Factor in an extra $1,000 to $3,000 to gussy up your home office for visiting clients.

INCOME

According to the CFP survey, the average planner makes $80,000, but veterans may earn $200,000 and up. Planners generate income through fees, commissions, or a combination of the two; they may bill by the hour or they may charge flat fees for specific services.

FOR MORE INFORMATION

• **The Institute of Certified Financial Planners** (ICFP) has 11,000 members and 75 local chapters. ICFP publishes a bimonthly journal and provides referrals (800-282-7526).

• **National Association of Personal Financial Advisers** (NAPFA) is an organization of fee-only planners. NAPFA publishes a monthly journal and provides referrals (888-FEE-ONLY).

• **International Association for Financial Planning** (IAFP) is open to anyone in the financial service business (800-945-4237).

• **The College of Financial Planning** in Denver offers a six-part CFP correspondence course, which takes about two years to complete and costs nearly $2,000 (303-220-4800).

• Local colleges and universities may also offer preparation courses for the CFP exam. Check your local Yellow Pages for colleges near you.

• **Certified Financial Planner Board of Standards** offers the 10-hour CFP exam (888-237-6275).

Management Consultant

Do you have a specific expertise in a hot area like health care or computers and a solid track record in the business world? Then you may be able to parlay your experience into a management consulting business. Of course, you'll also need to have razor-sharp problem-solving skills and the confidence to walk into an organization and give pointed (and not always welcome) advice on how to set the company on a better course.

The Bureau of Labor Statistics projects the number of management consultants will expand 35% by 2005. Why? American companies are under increasing pressure to compete in the global marketplace. They need objective experts to streamline operations, fine-tune marketing strategies, and tighten management operations. Specialization is crucial. Notes James H. Kennedy, publisher of *Consultants News*: "Highly focused consultants are prospering, while generalists are foundering."

Hot spots: Health care, information technology, and international trade.

SKILLS YOU NEED

A keen intellect, a strong ego, and the ability to work independently are essential. Consultants typically have a master of business administration (MBA) degree and five to 10 years of experience in the business world. The Institute of Management Consultants (see below) offers the certified management consultant (CMC) designation. To obtain the CMC you must have at least three years of experience, references, and take and pass a written exam. Insiders, though, say it adds little value.

The best credentials are experience. Information technology consultant Lee Greenhouse, for instance, worked for 15 years developing electronic products for big companies like E. F. Hutton and Citibank before going out on his own in 1992. Now he enjoys the intellectual stimulation of working on three to four projects at once. "I feel more valued as a hired gun," he says.

WORK-LIFE SNAPSHOT

Though you can look forward to big fees and challenging work, expect to put in long hours and spend as much as half your time on the road. "Constant contact with clients is critical," says Greenhouse. Some consultants, however, do manage to stay close to home. Cambridge-based consultant Paul O'Malley cultivates local Boston-area clients and only hops on planes a few times a month. When possible, O'Malley fine-tunes proposals with faraway clients via E-mail.

SPECIAL COSTS

All you need are a fast PC, a modem, a phone, and a fax line. Start-up costs can be as low as $2,000 if you already have a PC. You'll also need an E-mail program and access to the Internet for on-line research.

INCOME

A respected consultant in a hot area can earn up to $500,000. But the average income is closer to $100,000. Be patient: it could take you two to three years to rise into the lush six figures.

FOR MORE INFORMATION

• **The Institute of Management Consultants** (http://www.imcusa.org) publishes a biannual journal, and offers professional seminars and CMC certification ($250). Cost to join is $195 a year (212-697-8262).

• *Consultants News*. Started in 1970, this 12-page monthly newsletter offers news and tips for $188 a year (800-531-0007).

• The following books will help jump-start your business: *How to Become a Successful Consultant in Your Own Field* by Hubert Bermont ($12.95; Prima); *Million Dollar Consulting: The Professional's Guide to Growing a Practice* by Alan Weiss ($14.95, McGraw-Hill); and *How to Start and Run a Successful Consulting Business* by Gregory and Patricia Kishel ($15.95; John Wiley & Sons).

Manufacturer's Representative

"Manufacturer's representative" is fancy title for a salesperson. Instead of peddling products to the general public, however, the representative sells to other wholesalers, manufacturers, retailers, or government agencies, usually within a defined territory. Most reps work for several manufacturers, but they often deal with only one type of product. For instance, home-based entrepreneur Kelly Brown specializes in selling active sportswear lines to retailers in New England.

Thanks again to downsizing, more and more companies turn to commission-paid outside reps over a salaried in-house staff. Brown, for instance, grosses roughly $150,000 a year on a 7% commission. The average manufacturer's rep sold $3.9 million worth of goods in 1995, compared to $3.3 million in 1991—an 18% increase, according to a membership survey by the Manufacturer's Agents National Association (MANA).

Hot spots: Technology and pharmaceutical sales are strong growth areas, due to the fast pace of innovations. In both industries, reps tend to work exclusively for one company on a combined salary-and-commission pay structure.

SKILLS YOU NEED

Sales experience in a familiar industry gives you a leg up, but it's not a necessity. For instance, Suzy Murray became a manufacturer's rep right after she graduated from college with a degree in communications. During her career, she's jumped from the clothing industry to pharmaceuticals to software.

Most important, you must be a good, persuasive salesperson. Completing a sale may take months, so you need perseverance and patience, too. For help with such issues as selecting manufacturers to represent, negotiating a contract, developing a business plan, and learning sales skills, check out the seminars offered by MANA four times a year.

WORK-LIFE SNAPSHOT

While you may manage your business from home, expect to spend weeks on the road. MANA members say that their sales territories typically extend across five states. For instance, four times a year, when manufacturers introduce new sportswear lines, Brown travels throughout New England for six straight weeks. However, if she had a smaller, denser territory, she could probably sleep in her own bed every night.

SPECIAL COSTS

Travel takes the biggest bite out of a rep's budget, since so much time is spent on the road visiting buyers. You'll probably want to buy a laptop computer, too, with an internal fax modem for your on-the-road office. Subscribing to an on-line service is also helpful. "When I have appointments with companies, I like to visit their Web site and have some information when I go in," says Murray. "I'm on the Internet more than once a day." Finally, consider investing in a software program to keep you organized, such as REPS for Windows, which tallies your commissions, gives you sales graphs, and helps track orders.

INCOME POTENTIAL

Commissions range from 2% to 20% of sales, with higher percentages going to reps who sell extremely specialized products. The average income is $75,000 to $100,000, but top salespeople can earn $250,000 or more.

FOR MORE INFORMATION

• **MANA** offers members a monthly magazine, a membership directory, seminars, insurance, and travel discount programs. Membership costs $189 a year, with a $50 one-time initiation fee (714-859-4040).
• Subscribe to trade magazines covering the industry in which you specialize.

Market Research

Launching new products and services costs businesses billions of dollars every year. With so much at stake, companies must be certain that their new gizmo will be a success. So they turn to researchers to examine every aspect of the market before they make a move. These experts run focus groups to learn about consumer preferences, investigate competitors' sales strategies, determine how a product should be priced, and gather any data that could affect a company's success or failure.

Because the marketplace has become hypercompetitive, researchers are in sharp demand. In fact, the field should swell by 25% by the year 2005, according to the Bureau of Labor Statistics. What's more, to keep costs down, companies are increasingly likely to seek outside help, making market research a great business for home entrepreneurs.

Hot spots: Zeroing in on a specific industry—preferably one with which you are already well familiar—is the way to go. But if you opt to enter a new arena, the health-care field offers vast opportunity. The reason, as home entrepreneur Janet Pozen would tell you, is that anywhere there's change, there's a need for research. "Health care is in such a state of flux," she says, "that people have nothing but questions they need answered."

SKILLS YOU NEED

A good head for numbers and statistics is a definite plus. You also need to be adept at gaining people's trust, facilitating discussion, as well as listening and gleaning important observations. You don't need certification or a degree, but training is advisable. The Marketing Research Association offers a 12-month independent study program in conjunction with the University of Georgia, covering such topics as research design, sampling, data collection methods, measurement instruments, data analysis, and communicating research results ($399 for members, $599 for nonmembers, plus $160 for text books; 860-257-4008).

WORK-LIFE SNAPSHOT

If you primarily offer "qualitative" research, which typically involves running focus groups and gathering participants' emotional responses, you'll have to work evenings. You also may need to travel occasionally to gather information via face-to-face interviews. Or you can specialize in "quantitative" analysis, in which you do statistical studies by collecting data from telemarketing surveys, mailings, or the Internet.

SPECIAL COSTS

You'll have to plunk some money into survey and statistical analysis software. You should also subscribe to an on-line service that gives you access to information on your industry. Don't neglect to invest in a snappy software presentation package, too. After all, you'll need to deliver your findings in a clear, usable style for your clients.

INCOME POTENTIAL

Market researchers earn about $60,000 or so a year during the first several years. Once they're more established, they typically bring in around $100,000. Many do even better. For instance, Pam Danzinger, a home-based market researcher specializing in collectibles, pulls down $500,000 working for such well-known companies as Disney, Mattel, and Universal Studios.

FOR MORE INFORMATION

• Besides offering a 12-month course, the **Marketing Research Association** sends its 2,350 members a monthly newsletter and provides further training and support ($167 a year; 860-257-4008). For an additional $160, it will give you a listing in the Blue Book, an annual research service directory that companies use to look for pros.

• You should also subcribe to trade magazines in your industry, and keep tabs on mainstream business publications like *The Wall Street Journal*.

• Check out *American Demographics* magazine's Web site for free resources (http://www.marketingtools.com/).

Multimedia Designer

Each time you read a Web address like http://www.xxx.zzz, you're seeing a multimedia designer's handiwork. Multimedia designers create interactive materials that combine text, video, graphics, audio, music, and animation into products that educate or entertain. The most obvious examples are Web sites and CD-ROMS, but designers also create digital videodiscs and electronic kiosks. The vehicles are constantly evolving, but the final product is always accessed via computer.

As computer technology continues to advance at its current nanosecond pace, so too will the need for versatile designers who understand the capabilities of electronic media. According to the 1996 Worldwide Multimedia Forecast, the market for multimedia products and services will increase by 29% a year through the end of the decade.

Hot spots: Education and training for both academic and business applications.

SKILLS YOU NEED

You must be computer literate, but not necessarily a techno-wizard. It's also important to have an inquiring intellect and the ability to use sights and sounds to instruct or entertain. You should have at least one to two years of multimedia design experience, since most prospective employers will want to see samples of your work.

WORK-LIFE SNAPSHOT

If all this sounds too technical, take heart. Multimedia designers frequently start in print or graphic design and learn the technical skills in just a matter of years, sometimes even months. Ian List, an instructional designer, creates CD-ROM science study guides for college students. List's job is to take text blocks and images and turn them into interactive teaching tools. He needs to have an understanding of the technology, but he doesn't do any programming himself. "For me, the ability to teach through the features of the computer is the most important skill to have," he says.

One boon: You can do your job anywhere there's an adequate power supply—whether it's a mountaintop retreat or a beachside bungalow. Ronnie Fielding and Mark Feffer are partners in United Multimedia, a production company. They hire the designers, managers, and writers for each project from a cross-country network of specialists. On any given project, team members may never lay eyes on each other.

SPECIAL COSTS

You'll need a powerful PC with 16mg of RAM and a 2-gigabyte hard drive, a high-resolution screen, and a color printer. The total tab could be anywhere from $6,000 to $10,000. You'll also need multimedia development tool software and image processing software. Tip: You may be able to get equipment loans from clients. List's main client leased a Macintosh for him, gratis.

INCOME

In your first year, expect anywhere from $20,000 to $80,000, depending on how much work you bring in. Once you have a few years of experience, and a solid group of clients, you can easily pull down $100,000 to $150,000.

FOR MORE INFORMATION

• **International Interactive Communications Society** (IICS) is a good networking and information source. Started in 1983, the IICS has 36 chapters worldwide and an electronic monthly and quarterly newsletter. Membership costs $120 a year (503-620-3604) or go to their Web site (http://www.iics.org).

• **WebWeek** (http://www.webweek.com) offers news and technical information plus a handy articles-search feature (http://www.webweek.com/search).

• **UseNetNews.** A message board with over 25,000 groups. A good place to troll for updates on technical news, and to post queries. You can access UseNetNews via your Internet service provider.

• The **Software Publishers Association**'s Web site (http://www.spa) has interesting facts, figures, and surveys on the software industry as well as government reports.

• **CyberAtlas** (http://www.cyberatlas) offers great trend information on new media.

Public Relations Pro

Princess Di, President Clinton, small start-up companies, and large multinationals all employ specialists to shape and protect their public images. PR pros, as they're called, massage bad news like Whitewater developments and extramarital affairs and promote good news such as innovative new products and increased revenues. Besides polishing their clients' images, PR practitioners have become a critical communications and management tool for businesses.

The fact is, businesses today must maintain a high profile to survive, and that means that PR experts will be in increasing demand. The Bureau of Labor Statistics, in fact, predicts a 25% gain in this occupation by the year 2005.

Hot spots: Any industry undergoing change needs PR specialists to explain those shifts to a wary public. The medical field, for instance, holds lots of opportunity, largely because of the transformation spurred by managed care. Thanks to sweeping new regulations, the telecommunications industry is also undergoing changes that PR pros can explain and promote.

WORK-LIFE SNAPSHOT

You can live anywhere you want—a remote town in the mountains or New York City. However, it's a good idea to meet with your clients, particularly when you're first getting started. "There's no substitute for face-to-face meetings," says Nora Harrison, who runs her home business in Roseburg, Oregon, and travels one week every three months. Although you may have to field calls from the press at odd hours, in general, PR pros work a normal business day.

SKILLS YOU NEED

You must score a perfect 10 in communications. That means you need superb writing skills to harness the public's interest, poise in public speaking, finesse at dealing with all kinds of people and situations, and an eye for design to help you in making brochures and other publicity material. It's also essential to have a strong familiarity with the companies you represent.

Most pros end up specializing in one industry, or they offer a particular type of service, such as writing annual reports, doing television advertisements, or creating publicity kits. For instance, Harrison focuses on publishing newsletters, magazines, and brochures for her clients. Millie Szerman, on the other hand, offers a range of services, from designing creative product packaging to dealing with the media. But she specializes in one industry—gift manufacturers. Of course, many PR pros are generalists too. Judi Knapp, for instance, loves handling a variety of clients and projects. She promotes a woodwind quintet, works with political candidates, and digs embattled business owners out of bad holes.

SPECIAL COSTS

Besides splurging on high-quality marketing materials such as a colorful glossy brochure that describes your services, there are no out-of-the-ordinary costs.

INCOME POTENTIAL

PR pros take home an average of $50,000, but many of them do much better. If you have a few big clients that require regular services, you can easily earn six digits.

FOR MORE INFORMATION

• **The Public Relations Society of America** (PRSA) offers members professional development seminars, the use of the society's information center, as well as several regular publications, including *Public Relations Tactics* ($175 a year, plus a $65 initiation fee; 212-995-2230). It also has a training program and accreditation, called an APR for accredited public relations ($200 to take the exam).

• For an on-line directory of the nation's PR companies (plus links to many more sites), check out **Directory of Public Relations Agencies and Resources on the WWW** (http://www.impulse-research.com).

Systems Designer

From your local video store to the largest Fortune 500 conglomerate, computers are everywhere. And there's good reason: In today's competitive marketplace, computers are equivalent to speed, efficiency, and productivity. The systems designer's job is to develop procedures using computers and software to help organizations work more effectively. The designer's task may be as simple as choosing the right computer system for a start-up business to as complicated as designing customized software programs for a multinational corporation.

Systems designers can look forward to full dance cards. The Bureau of Labor Statistics predicts that demand for these specialists will increase by 92% through the year 2005, making it the third hottest job in the country after home-care and health-care aides.

Hot spots: Millennium systems designers who can help companies update their computers for the dates of the twenty-first century will be in demand. Con Edison, in New York, estimates the project will cost them $5 million. Another hot spot: designers who can convert companies from mainframes to PCs.

SKILLS YOU NEED

A thorough grasp of current computer technology and how it is developing is essential. You don't need a special degree, but you should have five or more years of experience on your résumé. The Institute for Certification of Computing Professionals (ICCP) offers the certified computing professional (CCP) degree, which may help if you're a novice. To earn the CCP you must have four years of work experience and pass three exams ($149 each). For more information check out the ICCP's home page (http://www.iccp.org) or call (847) 299-4227.

WORK-LIFE SNAPSHOT

The hours can be long and erratic. Most designers spend normal business hours at the client's office and then return home to work out problems and do research. Though designers are typically hired to work on one-time projects that last anywhere from several weeks to several years, many maintain long-term relationships with clients. Ernest Fine, who specializes in small companies, has ongoing relationships with 10 clients.

SPECIAL COSTS

There's no escaping it. You'll have to shell out big bucks. You'll need two PCs to test networking systems plus equipment and software that mimics that of your major clients. It's essential to be hooked up to the Internet to conduct research and communicate with clients. Total tab: $5,000 to $10,000.

INCOME

Designers with a few years of experience typically make $75,000 a year. But it's not uncommon for take-home pay to reach $250,000. Fine, in business since 1993, earns about $150,000 a year.

FOR MORE INFORMATION

• **Independent Computer Consultants Association** (ICCA) was founded in 1976 and has 1,500 members and 23 chapters. Members use the organization as a networking tool; the ICCA also has a newsletter and holds a national conference. Annual fee is $160 a year (800-774-4222). For more information go to their Web site (http://www.icca.org).

• **WebWeek** (http://www.webweek.com). News and technical information plus a handy articles-search feature (http://www.webweek.com/search).

• **UseNetNews.** A message board with over 25,000 groups. A good place to troll for updates on technical news, and to post queries. You can access UseNetNews via your Internet service provider.

• **Software Publishers Association.** The SPA's Web Site (http://www.spa.org) has interesting facts, figures, and surveys on the software industry as well as government reports.

Temporary Help Provider

Manpower, Inc., the granddaddy of the temp business, is now one of the nation's largest employers. No wonder. As corporate America has been paring its payrolls and adjusting to a rapidly changing workplace, the need for highly skilled temporary workers has increased dramatically. According to the National Association of Temporary and Staffing Services, the number of temporary workers nearly doubled from 1991 through 1995 to 2.2 million—or nearly 2% of the total workforce. Temporary-help agency revenues rose from $20.5 billion to $39.2 billion over the same time period. Erase your image of the Kelly Girl. These days temp workers come from all walks of professional life and include architects, systems designers, psychologists, and even troubleshooting executives. The temporary-help provider's mission is to supply businesses with these seasoned pros or basic support staff on a daily, weekly, or monthly basis.

Hot spots: information technology and professional services.

SKILLS YOU NEED

Pick a specialty you know inside and out. Les Kalmus had 28 years of experience in information technology before he started CyberStaff, a computer temp agency. Besides an industry specialty, you must be organized, diplomatic, and have good business smarts. "This is basically a sales job," notes Kalmus.

WORK-LIFE SNAPSHOT

Most of your time will be spent screening and interviewing potential employees. Expect to spend a few days a week away from your office to meet with clients and make site visits. Warning: It may be difficult to maintain a *growing* temp business in your home. Many providers bust out of their home office within a year. Les and Barbara Kalmus started CyberStaff in their New York City apartment. Within six months, the business was going great guns, and they were ready to relocate.

SPECIAL COSTS

Start-up costs are minimal. In fact, all you need is a phone, a fax, a professional answering service, and a PC. Once business gets going, you'll need a database program to monitor employees and clients. If clients or job applicants will be coming to your home, add $1,000 to $3,000 to your budget for sprucing up your home office.

INCOME

The average temporary-help business with 32 employees makes about $150,000 in annual profits, according to Genesis Services Group. Providers typically bill clients 30% to 50% more than they pay employees. If you're in a hot area, profits can be higher. CyberStaff pulled in revenues of $2.5 to $3 million in its second year of business.

FOR MORE INFORMATION

• **National Association of Temporary and Staffing Services** (NATSS) has 1,500 members and offers publications, seminars, and a start-up reference kit for $50. Membership dues are based on sales, but the minimum is $240 a year (703-549-6287) or visit their Web site (http://www.natss.com/staffing).

• **Genesis Services Group** (http://www.genesisgroup.com) is a for-profit group that assists temporary help businesses with training, consulting, and financial advice, among other services (800-694-9997).

CHAPTER 3

Create a Financial Foundation

You've probably heard those ominous stats about business start-up failures, the ones that say that five out of six new enterprises don't make it to their six-year anniversary. Well, those stats are indeed correct. True, in recent years business-failure rates have been falling, but starting a new business is *still* risky, and many operations that start with great ideas and top talent never take off. Why? Talk to any banker or small business expert and they'll tell you the almost universal reason is lack of capital and poor planning. You may have the idea of the century or the know-how of a maestro, but if you can't finance your dream and keep it going, you could find your business careening toward bankruptcy in no time. If you want your business to truly soar—and not just squeak by from year to year—proper financial planning is essential.

But you need more than just cash in the bank. You need a budget and a realistic plan. So in this chapter we'll show you how to:

- Project your financial needs
- Draw up a detailed business plan
- Find money from your own assets and your network of family and friends
- Convince lenders to finance you
- Locate free advice to help you get started

Project Your Financial Needs

How much cash do you need to get going? To answer that question, you need to figure out both your one-time start-up costs and your ongoing monthly expenses. You want to know at the outset how much money you need to get your business up and running *and* how much it will take to keep the business purring all year long. At the same time think about what your *personal* needs are. How much salary do you need to draw from the business to pay your kids' preschool bills and cover your household expenses?

By anticipating as many of your financial needs as you can at the outset, you'll be able to avoid cash crises down the line that could slow up business and add extra stress in your crucial first year. What's more, banks, and even your friends, are less likely to lend you money when your business is teetering on insolvency than when it is poised to soar.

To get an idea of what your first-year expenses will be, talk to other home business owners in your field. When Beverly Rose was considering starting a secretarial services business, she posed questions on CompuServe's Working From Home Forum (GO WORK). "People were so helpful in telling me what to expect," she says. Rose was warned, for instance, to consider hefty professional fees to accountants and computer consultants during her first year. She was also told to set aside money for the inevitable equipment breakdowns. Ask colleagues what their biggest unforeseen expenses were and when cash flow dried up—and why. From your market research (see Chapter 1) you should have an idea of the demand for your product or service and when demand will be strong and when it will be soft.

Remember Murphy's Law: If something can go wrong, it will. Err on the side of caution and overestimate your expenses and underestimate your income for your first year. Each home business is different, but it is not unusual for it to take a year or more for your business to turn a profit. One way to approach your first budget is to create two versions: an optimistic one and a pessimistic one. Make sure you can survive through both scenarios.

First, **estimate your start-up costs**—the funds you will need to get your business up and running. It's not unusual to start a home business on just a few thousand dollars. Beverly Rose, for instance, needed only $1,000 to get her secretarial business up to full speed. Consider all your requirements before you set up shop. What about legal fees, special software, or a speedy new modem? The worksheet below will help you brainstorm start-up costs.

START-UP COSTS

Furniture and fixtures
Equipment
Remodeling or
    redecorating
Initial promotional
    expenses
Legal and accounting
    fees
Starting inventory
Licenses and permits
Cash
Miscellaneous

Total

Next, **create a cash flow chart for your first year of business.** This statement shows—month by month—how much money will be coming into the business, how much will be going out, and when those events will happen. For instance, quarterly taxes and health-insurance premiums may come due at the same time, leaving you in a cash crunch if you haven't planned ahead. Your cash flow statement will help you budget throughout the year and determine if you need to borrow money at a specific time of the year. You can use the form below or buy a software package such as Quick Books (Intuit: 800-446-8848) to help you work up a plan. The format is not important. What is crucial, though, is to focus on financial forecasting *before* you start your business.

CASH FLOW

	Jan.	Feb.	Mar.	April	May	June	July	Aug.	Sept.	Oct.	Nov.	Dec.

Income
Cash sales
Credit sales
Other income
Total income

Expenses
Cost of goods
VARIABLE
 EXPENSES:
Marketing
Selling
 expenses
Supplies
Transportation

CASH FLOW

	Jan.	Feb.	Mar.	April	May	June	July	Aug.	Sept.	Oct.	Nov.	Dec.
FIXED												
EXPENSES												
Insurance												
Taxes												
Your salary												
Utilities												
Legal &												
professional												
fees												
Loan &												
interest												
payments												
Total Expenses												
Cash Balance												

Once you've made a good effort at estimating your financials, run your numbers by an accountant who's worked with small business owners or another small business pro (see box on page 71 on how to find a low-cost consultant) to make sure your projections are on track.

Draw Up a Solid Business Plan

Drafting a detailed business plan is a critical step on your path to success. You might think, I've got it all figured out in my head, I don't need to write anything down. Okay. But research shows that the act of writing, whether it is a business plan or a daily to-do list, gives you a stronger sense of commitment. Robert Cialdini, a professor of psychology at Arizona State University and author of *Influence: The Psychology of Persuasion*, says putting pen to paper makes you take yourself more seriously. And that increases your chances of achieving your goals.

Aside from increasing your personal sense of commitment, there are two practical reasons you need a *written* plan: (1) to get funding from lenders and (2) to help you focus on your company's goals. Before they'll take a risk on you, lenders need to know who you are, how profitable you could become, and what's unique about your service or product. As a business owner, you need to stand back and take an objective look at your own enterprise: its strengths and weaknesses, competitors, and long-term goals. Writing a plan will pull together all your assorted ideas, schemes, and dreams into one powerful blueprint.

Of course, many small start-ups begin on a whim, a prayer, and a few hundred dollars—and no formal plan. This is not the best strategy. For instance, Jeff Yoak, an Internet development trainer in Florida, started his business in a spare bedroom with "lots of great ideas and a real interest and love for technology"—but no long-term plan. Lucky for him, Yoak Enterprises took off. A year into business, Yoak was already getting bigger jobs. Concerned about how he would handle more work, he decided it was time to get focused. So he began drafting a six-month and one-year plan. "A business plan is a tool to make sure [my ideas] are practical and financially doable," says Yoak. By writing down the projects he worked on and how much he was paid, Yoak saw some holes in his operation. He decided he was "branching off too much," and wasting time on small-fry projects, like designing Web sites, which he could easily hire someone else to do. His unique talent was in interactive programming, which was five times more profitable.

Yoak's plan focused on short-term goals. But if you're looking for financing, most banks will want to see farther down the road and will require a one-year plan and a three-year plan. You don't need a twenty-page tome. For starters five to ten pages will do. The plan should include (but not necessarily be limited to) the following sections. You will have to customize the document to suit your particular business.

Company description. Right away, explain what business you're in and what makes your company unique. Then give the essential details: where you will be located, what your specific product or service is, and what the company will be called. State the legal form (see chapter 5) that the business will take: sole proprietorship, C corporation, or S corporation. If you will have employees or partners, list them here.

Management. Make hay out of your credentials. If you're just starting out and have no previous business experience, convince skeptical lenders why they should take a gamble on you. Says small business consultant Gene Fairbrother, "Banks are not lending to a business, they are lending to a person. If they don't think you're qualified, they won't give you the loan." Prove you have the experience, know-how, and personality to make your idea into a profitable reality. List your education, your past employment, and any entrepreneurial experience you have had. If you have a partner, employees, or a board of directors, explain who they are and what experience they will bring to the business.

Products or services. Describe in detail the unique nature of your product or service. What will make it stand apart from the competition? If you are making a product, spell out the manufacturing process and anything that is unusual about it. For instance: Is it safer for the environment than similar products? Does it use rare parts or ingredients? If you are providing a service, explain what new twist you will bring to the marketplace.

Market. In this section, explain why there is a need for your business. Back up your claims with statistics when possible. For instance, if you are opening a financial planning practice, show how much the field is projected to grow. Also, describe your local market. Is there a dearth of financial planners in your area?

Is there a growing influx of retirees who will need your services? The Bureau of Labor Statistics produces figures on how quickly professions are expanding. And the Census Bureau puts out reports that project regional economic expansion (http://www.census.gov). These are great sources to not only prove a growing need, but also to help you research your market potential. (See Chapter 1 for more information on researching your market.)

Competition. Discuss your competitors and how you will stand apart. Answer these questions: What companies will you be competing with directly? What products do they offer? What customer base do they serve? What are their strengths and weaknesses? Now explain how your business will be better. Will you offer friendlier service? lower prices? savvier knowledge? faster delivery? Will you occupy a niche that is being underserved? When Mike Waters was developing his software product, Congress Merge, a program that helps lobbyists identify specific members of Congress, he faced two direct competitors. "One company's product was overpriced and difficult to use," he says. "The other was lower priced but did not offer an instruction manual." Waters explained in his business plan that his product would cost less than the high-end product, but provide more service than the low-end competitor.

Marketing strategy. Identify your target audience and describe in detail how you plan to reach your potential customers. Do you already have a stable of clients from your last job or will you start from scratch? Do you have a network of professionals who can help market your service? Will you be advertising, and if so where and how? Will you be doing direct-mail campaigns, making cold calls, or selling your product or service via your new Web site? Show that you've thought through all the details.

Financing. Demonstrate a thorough understanding of your company's financial needs: how much cash you need to get started and where will it come from. Include your annual cash flow statement and a balance sheet that shows your assets and liabilities.

If all this sounds overwhelming, by all means call on an expert for help. The box on page 71 will tell you how to find free or low-cost consulting advice. There are also a number of books and software programs that can provide you with a basic business-plan blueprint. The Internet also is a good place to learn more about business plans. Just remember to make your plan unique. Canned language or cookie-cutter proposals can send up a red flag to lenders that you simply "filled in the blanks" and don't understand the intricacies of your business.

FOR MORE INFORMATION

• Bulletin 2472, *Employment Outlook: 1994–2005*. U.S Government Printing Office, Superintendent of Documents, Mail Stop:SSOP, Washington, D.C. 20402-9328.
• *How to Write a Winning Business Plan* by Joseph Mancuso ($15.00; Fireside).
• BizPlan Builder (Jian; 800-346-5426) a software program that takes you through the writing process, step by step.
• The Small Business Administration publishes a free pamphlet *How to Start a Home Based Business* (SBA Answer Desk, 800-8ASKSBA). The SBA Web site also has information on writing business plans (http://www.sbaonline.sba.gov).
• Check out local colleges and adult education centers for courses on business plan writing.

Tap into Financing Close to Home

Realistically, most of the money for your new business will come from your own back pocket or those of your loved ones. In fact, 95% of all small business start-ups, including those based in the home, are financed by a creative combination of personal money, family loans, and credit cards, according to the Small Business Administration. Using personal assets is a fine way to get your business started. You have more control over your money and you can avoid dealing with bank red tape. What's more, most banks will not loan money to a small business unless the owner has contributed a significant amount, say 30% to 40%, of his or her own personal funds. But homespun financing can be fraught with perils. Your spouse may not agree about raiding your mutual fund, and family relations can be strained when you take out a loan from a relative. So before you begin drawing down cash, take a look at *all* the options you have available close to home and select the ones that will put the least strain on your finances and personal relations.

YOUR OWN MONEY

In our credit-happy society, you have access to more cash than you probably know. Tap into your checking account overdraft line and open up a few new credit cards and you could have $100,000 or more to fund your company. You may even be able to borrow against your spouse's retirement account. But first think of the long-term ramifications of borrowing. Interest rates on credit cards are typically sky high, for instance. Rule of thumb: Start by using the cheapest money first—like your own savings or borrowing against your investments.

Savings. If you have a sizable chunk of cash stashed in a mutual fund or CDs and it's not earmarked for your retirement or your kids' college education, spend this money first. You pay no interest on the funds and you have easy access to the cash. But leave enough for an emergency. The conventional wisdom says you should have three months' worth of living expenses in reserve, but if you are the only one bringing home the bacon or your business has a long ramp-up time, then you might indeed need six to twelve months' worth of living expenses in an emergency fund.

WHERE TO GET FREE (AND ALMOST FREE) BUSINESS ADVICE

There are a number of resources that can provide assistance in everything from refining your business plan to drafting your financial statements to implementing a marketing plan—for no fee or a very nominal one. Just make sure that when seeking advice from strangers, you ask for their credentials first. No advice is better than the person giving it. And free help can cost you in the long run if it sets you off on the wrong track.

Service Corps of Retired Executives (SCORE). Created by the SBA in 1964, SCORE is comprised of retired executives who provide free counseling to small business owners. There are about 12,600 SCORE volunteers in 389 chapters across the country. Volunteers must take a "counselor professional development program" and sign a statement of ethics before they can give advice. Most branches work closely with the local chamber of commerce. While in theory SCORE is a great concept, the quality of volunteers is uneven. Some of these well-meaning execs may have been out of the workforce for a number of years and may be unfamiliar with your particular business. Before you start working with a SCORE volunteer, quiz the person about his or her background and experience with home-based businesses. Mike Waters says he received "invaluable" help from SCORE. The volunteer he worked with had been a chief financial officer at a consumer products corporation. "The volunteer helped me fine-tune my business plan and pointed out potential risks, such as the threat of litigation." You can also ask for team counseling, which will give you two professionals to work with. The SCORE headquarters are in Washington (1030 15th Street NW, Washington, D.C. 20005; 202-653-6958/6279 or 800-8ASK-SBA). Additionally, call your local chamber of commerce for information on the local SCORE office or place a request for help on the SBA Web site (http://www.sba.gov).

Small Business Development Centers (SBDC). SBDCs offer both training and counseling to small business owners. These centers are funded in part by the SBA and receive additional money from local colleges, businesses, and private donors. Most of the 1,000 centers are located at local community colleges or universities. Though there may be a small fee for training courses ($20 to $75), counseling is usually free. Through courses and one-on-one counseling, you can learn how to draft a business plan, research your market, and find sources of local financing. SBDC consultants are specialists in small business and tend to be a bit more savvy than SCORE volunteers. To find an SBDC near you, call your local SBA district office, the SBA hotline (800-8ASK-SBA) or the Association of Small Business Development Centers (703-448-6124).

National Business Incubation Association (NBIA). There are over 500 business incubators across the country designed to help new companies get up and running. Like the name implies, incubators are actual sites where small businesses can rent cheap space during their critical start-up phase. The centers also offer training, counseling, and networking opportunities. Most incubators will extend their services to off-site businesses (like yours) as well. To find one near you, send a SASE to NBIA, 20 East Circle Drive, Suite 190, Athens, OH 45701 or call up the NBIAs Web site (http://www.nbia.org) for a list of incubators by state.

Graduate Business Schools. If you are willing to be a guinea pig for a business or marketing class, you may be able to get your local university or college graduate business school to help you formulate a business or marketing plan. You get the benefit of their expertise for free, and they get to learn more about the real-life dilemmas of a home-based business owner. Call up your local university to see if they are interested in working with you. At the very least they may be able to refer you to an experienced graduate student who can help for a small fee.

Association for Enterprise Opportunity (AEO). The AEO can help you locate a micro-enterprise development organization in your area. These grassroots nonprofits provide low-cost training and assistance to economically disadvantaged small business start-ups. They can help you write your business plan as well as locate alternative sources of funding (312-357-0177).

Retirement accounts. We do not advise raiding your retirement accounts to start your business. But if you're young, say under 35, with plenty of time to rebuild your savings, and your 401(k) or IRA is your *only* source of cash, well then okay. Just remember that you'll be leveraging your current business prospects against your future livelihood. You could also lose as much as half the money right off the top for early-withdrawal penalties and taxes. The IRS will charge you a 10% early withdrawal fee and levy income taxes due on the money. A better option is to tap your spouse's retirement savings plan, like a 401(k) or 403(b), if he or she has one. Most plans will let you take out a loan of up to half the value of the account. There is no penalty to the IRS, since you'll be replacing the money, and you pay the interest back to yourself, not a bank. But be forewarned: If your spouse has any plans to cut loose and join you in business, remember the loan will have to be paid back in full before he or she quits. Unfortunately, you cannot borrow against your IRA.

Home equity loans. If you're a homeowner with sufficient equity in your home, then you have a ready form of cash. You can take out a loan for up to about 80% of the value of your house, including your first mortgage. The beauty of HELs is that—unlike a commercial loan—you don't have to explain what you are using the money for and the rates are low because your home is considered reliable collateral. What's more, the interest is tax deductible on amounts up to $100,000. Tip: If you're a sole proprietor, deposit the money into your company's checking account and deduct the interest on Schedule C as a business expense. By deducting it from your business rather than your personal tax return, you'll be able to save an additional 15.3% on self-employment taxes. But don't jeopardize your future. Make sure you can always make your minimum payments and don't borrow every possible dime. That way if, God forbid, your business fails and you end up defaulting on the loan, you won't lose your house and your business in one fell swoop.

Margin loans. If you're not comfortable liquidating your portfolio, or it's earmarked for retirement or your kids, consider borrowing against your holdings. You can borrow against up to 50% of the value of your stocks and bonds and most of your mutual funds (note: some brokers won't let you borrow against volatile-sector or -country funds). The rates on margin loans tend to be as much as one percentage point lower than personal loans, since securities can be easily liquidated. The big risk with margin loans, though, is that if the market drops and you suddenly have more than 50% of your portfolio outstanding, you must either come up with more cash pronto or sell your securities. To safeguard against a market downturn, borrow only up to 25% of your total portfolio.

Credit cards. According to Dun & Bradstreet, the major source of funding for small businesses in 1995 was not their local bank, but their own credit cards. Small wonder. Credit cards are easy to get, and you don't have to fill out lengthy loan forms to explain what you will be using the money for. What's more, plastic is a ready and unsecured form of money. If you can't pay, no one can come and repossess your home or car. But a word of warning: If you plan to apply for a bank loan, don't apply for numerous cards at once. Your fervor will appear on your credit report and send a signal to lenders that you may be overextended. And while plastic is a simple way to get your business going, it can be a costly one, too. Since interest rates can get up into the double digits, that computer you bought for $2,500 could easily turn into a $5,000 PC if you make only the minimum payments on your balance. One way to get around the high fees is to shop for a low-rate card. For a $4 fee, Bankcard Holders of America (524 Branch Drive, Salem, VA 24153) will send you a quarterly list of the 50 cards with the lowest rates. And look for superlow teaser rates offered by banks to lure you to their cards. Once they raise their rates—typically after six months or a year—then quickly switch your balance to another carrier with a competitive rate.

FAMILY AND FRIENDS' MONEY

A logical place to turn for start-up cash (after you've depleted your own) is your network of family and friends. This is a potential land mine, so tread lightly. If your business founders you risk ruining a friendship or creating family discord. On the other hand, if the business does swimmingly, you will have shared the start-up of your enterprise with those dearest to you. To stave off conflict, approach loved ones who not only have cash to spare, but who also have some business know-how and are familiar with terms like liability, cash flow, and depreciation. If the business has troubles and your payments are late, you'll at least be able to explain why. Here are three key strategies to make sure your deal remains amicable.

Decide on terms. You have three basic options: asking for a loan, offering an equity stake, or requesting a gift. A *loan* is the most straightforward. You decide on the amount you need, a fair interest rate, and a repayment schedule. Make sure that you set a realistic repayment plan that won't strain your cash flow. Small increments over a long period are safest.

With an *equity stake*, you sell a piece of your business. The investor/friend receives a percentage of your company and any profits or losses associated with it. The upside: You don't have to pay anyone back. The downside: You lose complete control. You have to decide if you can handle having a partner with a financial stake in your new business.

Lastly, you can request an outright *gift*. One way is to ask your parents for an advance on your inheritance. Or simply ask relatives for small contributions of just $500 or so. This is the least stressful approach, and family members are often happy to contribute small amounts of seed money to a good cause—your new business!

Get it in writing. No matter what terms you decide on, draw up a written agreement. Be sure it includes the date of the loan and the total amount you are borrowing, the payment schedule, interest rate, and date the loan will be paid in full. It's smart to have a plan B. Spell out what will happen if you fall behind in payments or are unable to pay back the full amount. Both parties should sign the document.

Set boundaries. Lastly, establish guidelines about when business can and cannot be discussed. You don't want to ruin a family reunion with a heated discussion about why you decided to lease, not buy, a business car, or whether it's smart to take out a margin loan against your kids' college fund. Draw clear lines and stick to them.

Look to Commercial Lenders

Good news (or at least better news): Just five years ago banks looked skeptically on home-based businesses and considered them fly-by-night enterprises. But now, as homegrown operations have begun sprouting up by the thousands across the country, and have been doing quite well, banks are giving them a second look. However, since start-ups still have a high failure rate, bank loans are still tricky to land. Commercial lenders want to be sure there is a steady stream of income from which repayments can be made. Plus, they want a backup form of collateral in case the business fails—equipment or real estate, for instance, which small start-ups often lack. Moreover, most lenders aren't interested in handing out small-time loans under $10,000, the amount home-based businesses typically need. That's because it costs as much for a bank to process a $10,000 loan as a $100,000 loan, yet the small loan will throw off much less income for the bank.

To overcome the odds, proper planning is essential. One of the main reasons entrepreneurs get turned down for financing is poor prep work, says David Burden, associate director of Small Business Banking at the American Bankers Association. Too often, businesspeople walk into a bank with no financial statements to make their case. Moreover, they don't fully understand how bank lending works. So before you go knocking at a bank door, follow these five key steps:

1. **Establish a relationship.** Make friends with a loan officer at your local bank while you still have your day job. Tell him or her of your plans to start a business and discuss ways that the bank can help. If your local bank is not amenable to business loans, ask other entrepreneurs for references to bankers. Or call your local chamber of commerce for recommendations. Once your business begins to grow, you can turn to your banker for advice on how to expand and where to find the cash. Many small business owners even invite their banker to see their home office or new product. Terri Lonier, author of *Working Solo* and *The Frugal Entrepreneur*, sends her banker postcards when she's on the road for business. "I want the bank to know I'm doing well," she says.

2. **Know what you need.** Figure out how much money you need and for what purposes. Then discuss with your banker what method of financing makes most sense for you. For instance, banks typically will not lend seed money for a new business, but will lend money for new equipment. If you foresee a cash flow crunch at specific times of the year, a line of credit may be more appropriate than a standard term loan. If you need less than $10,000, ask about a loan guaranteed by the SBA (see below). Banks are most comfortable making large loans for short periods, like two to five years, so they can earn big interest without much risk.

3. **Prove you can repay.** Your cash flow statement should prove that you will have adequate funds to make your loan payments. Seems like a Catch-22. If you had great cash flow, why would you be at the bank in first place? Show then that the money you borrow will help increase business and hence boost your profitability. You must reassure the skittish bank that if your business heads south, you have some form of collateral to liquidate—like a piece of real estate or equipment. If you do not have that collateral in your business, you will have to

sign a personal guarantee or find a wealthy friend to co-sign the loan.

4. **Show that you have the right stuff.** You can probably prove that you have the talent and drive of an entrepreneur (otherwise, why would you be starting up your own biz?). But as a one-person show, can you also manage cash flow, market your service or product, and keep your business growing long term? If your banker asks you a financial question, don't point to your business plan's financial statement and say, "Um, my accountant did that." That's a red alert to a loan officer that you lack financial savvy. Another sign of naïveté is that you are relying on just one customer or one supplier. If that customer backs out or your supplier goes dry, your business could fall apart in a matter of months. It's the classic eggs-in-one-basket scenario, and it makes bankers very nervous.

5. **Have the backup to prove it.** This is where your business plan comes in. You need to point to hard evidence that you can put your money (or their money, in this case) where your mouth is. Be able to explain in detail your marketing and advertising plan and point out your unique expertise outlined in your biography. Are you a member of the local chamber of commerce, an officer in your trade group, or an adjunct professor at the local community college? Anything that proves your business know-how helps speed up the lending process.

Small Business Administration (SBA) Loans

The SBA was created in 1953 by an act of Congress to help fund and support small businesses. Among their many offerings, including training and counseling programs, the SBA has a variety of loan programs for start-ups and existing small businesses. In their first 40 years, the government agency approved 625,000 loans totaling $80 billion. Not bad. But the agency historically has had a bad rep for being slow and cumbersome. In recent years the SBA has cleaned up its act, though, and it now boasts an average turnaround time of just six business days on loan guarantees. Even better, the SBA began new loan programs in the early '90s to meet the needs of microbusinesses—many of them home based—that needed miniloans that banks were reluctant to grant. So even if you've heard derogatory remarks about the SBA, don't let that stand between you and a potentially great lending source.

Before we explain the loans programs suitable for home-based businesses, here's a little background on the SBA. First, the SBA is not a bank. In almost all cases, the SBA does not directly lend money, instead they *guarantee* bank loans. Say you walk into your local bank and ask for five grand to open a consulting business in your garage. But the bank says, "No way José, we don't lend seed money and we don't lend paltry amounts." Then ask if the bank would make the loan if the SBA would guarantee it. Virtually all banks are approved SBA lenders. If the banks says yes, it will then forward your paperwork to the SBA.

As a guarantor, the SBA's rules are a little less strict than a regular bank. "We are more willing to take risks than a bank," says Michael Dowd, director in the Office of Loan Programs at the SBA. In fact one-third of SBA loans are granted to start-up businesses. The SBA, for instance, does not insist that you have a secondary form of collateral. What's more, the SBA is more willing to grant long-term loans. The average bank loan is three to seven years; the average SBA loan is 11 to 12 years, and they will go up to 25 years for real estate loans.

To qualify for an SBA loan, you must meet certain requirements: You must operate for profit, not be a far-out, speculative business—like an oil wildcatter—and meet the definition of "small" for your field. For instance, a service business must have average annual gross receipts of less than $5 million for the past three years—probably not a limit you'll have difficulty staying within at the outset.

If you've had difficulty securing bank financing, or you are a member of a minority or are disabled, SBA loans are worth investigating. Call your local SBA loan office and request a loan kit, which includes a list of programs, an application, and qualification requirements.

The most popular loans for home-based businesses are:

• **7(a) Guaranteed loans.** The original SBA loan program named for the section of the 1953 Small Business Act that authorized loans, "7(a)s" account for 80% of all loans granted by the agency. These are big-time loans and can be guaranteed for up to $750,000. About 95% of banks are authorized to process 7(a)s. But the process is lengthy. In addition to the regular bank forms, you have to fill out a six-to-eight-page application for the SBA. The maximum term is 10 years, unless you are applying for a real estate loan, then it can be up to 25 years. Interest rates are capped at 2.75 points above the prime rate.

• **LowDoc loans.** If you need less than $100,000, LowDocs offer less hassle. The application form is just one page, hence the name ("low documentation"). Created in 1993, LowDocs are a type of 7(a) and now comprise half of all 7(a) loans. Approval comes in a speedy two to three days. Though you can apply for a longer loan, the average is granted for 5.5 years. The interest rate is negotiable between you and the bank, but there are some limits. If the loan is for over seven years, the maximum the bank can charge is prime plus 2.25%.

• **Microloans.** This pilot program was started in 1993 to offer small loans (the maximum is $25,000) to local businesses. Unlike 7(a) loans, microloans are administered by local non-profit organizations—not banks. In 1996 there were 102 outfits offering microloans for amounts as small as $450. The average loan size was $10,450, with an average maturity of 44 months. To find the name of a lender in your locale, call the SBA microloan office at 202-205-7523 or call your local SBA office.

• **Fastrak loans.** The latest offering from the SBA, the Fastrak is the FedEx of the SBA's loan program. There is no paperwork, and, if approved, you can get your mitts on up to $100,000 in up to 48 hours. But only 18 lenders currently offer these loans. What's more, you need a squeaky clean credit rating to qualify. Again, call your local SBA office to find a lender near you.

• **Women's Prequalification Pilot Loan Program.** If you suspect that lenders are snubbing your loan application because you're a woman, this program can help. Basically, the SBA provides you with a commitment letter good for 30 days that states you're "okay." You can then take that to a commercial lender as a guarantee. The loan can be no more than $250,000, and your business must be 51% owned and operated by women. You must meet the same credit requirements as for 7(a) loans. The program was started in 1994, so there are just a few dozen outfits that participate in the program. Call your local SBA office to find an intermediary near you.

Some final tips, verbatim from the SBA:

• **Take cash flow seriously.** The most important document in your business plan is the monthly cash flow statement. It numerically represents the research in your narrative. Be sure that the numbers are clear and well conceived.

• **Avoid optimism.** Think carefully about your ideal repayment term and avoid being overly optimistic. Remember that you can always opt to pay your loan back faster, but it is difficult to do the reverse.

• **Have a stake in the business.** The SBA wants proof of your commitment. Typically they want to see that you have contributed about 30% to 35% of your own cash to your new business. Plus, they'll want to see that the business plan is well researched and makes sense.

• **Be prepared to provide personal guarantees.** The SBA frequently requires that you pledge personal property (like your house) if you do not have collateral to cover the entire loan.

FOR MORE INFORMATION

• *Mancuso's Small Business Basics* by Joseph Mancuso ($9.95; Sourcebooks).

• *Borrowers Guide*, a pamphlet on SBA loans (800-8ASKSBA).

• The SBA's Web site (www.sbaonline.sba.gov) has a wealth of information on their loans programs.

• *The Financial Success Source Book* ($1.75 from the American Bankers Association; 800-338-0626) provides basic financing tips.

• *Finding Money for Your Small Business* by Max Fallek ($19.95, Enterprise Dearborn; 800-829-7934).

• *Loan Builder* (Jian; 800-346-5426), a software program that helps you analyze your financial needs and identifies lending sources.

CHAPTER 4

Getting Ready for Business

You've nailed your winning idea and secured your finances; now you're ready for business. Well, almost. Before you start wooing clients you need to give your enterprise a firm base. That includes creating an efficient home office loaded with time-saving equipment and securing adequate insurance to safeguard yourself against a calamity. In addition, you'll want to reestablish those cushy health and retirement benefits you had at your old job.

Sounds expensive, right? Not necessarily. You needn't bust your bottom line to get started. Furniture can be found on the cheap, and high-powered computers and speedy fax machines are more affordable than ever. Even pricey health insurance policies, which used to scare most nine-to-fivers away from self-employment, are more affordable thanks to the Health Insurance Portability and Accountability Act of 1996, which allows you to deduct a bigger portion of your premiums.

In this chapter, we'll cover:

- Furnishing and equipping your home office
- Buying business insurance
- Finding the right health, life, and disability coverage
- Choosing the best tax-deferred retirement savings plan

Find the Right Space

The dining room table just won't cut it as operation central for your new business. To create the most productive and inspiring office space, you need a room of your own, preferably one about 12 feet by 12 feet that is dedicated to your business and nothing else. But it's not just a matter of comfort. It's much easier to claim the home-office deduction if you have a dedicated office with a door (for more on tax deductions see Chapter 5).

If you plan to see clients on the premises, a ground-floor office is preferable—that way they won't have to tromp through your personal space. If it's just you on your own, then any area of the home will be fine, as long as it's worker friendly. Your office could be a corner of the basement or attic, a spare bedroom, or even your garage. But, before you set yourself up, spend some time in the space. Are there distracting noises from outside? Can you hear the neighbor's dog barking or the TV blaring from the family room? Is there enough ventilation, and are there sufficient outlets for you to plug in all your high-tech gear? Your office should be comfortable, well lit, and quiet: a place where you can shut the door to kids, cats, and the din of family life.

Furnish It Simply

It's easy to get seduced by $1,200 swivel chairs and executive suite desk sets. But take it easy at the get-go. You'll need your cash for more important things down the line (like—ho-hum—medical bills, business cards, and marketing brochures). Make a detailed list of all the items you'll need (consult the list below) and then figure out how to find them at a cut rate. You should aim to get the best furniture and equipment you can afford. If you shop wisely you won't have to go into debt to do so.

For starters, scour the used-office-furniture stores in your neighborhood. Also, look in the business section of your local paper for office-furniture auctions. (Be sure to call for the specs before you go; some auctions set minimums on how much you must spend.) Another source of high-quality used equipment is classified ads in your paper. Look under "Merchandise for Sale." Office discount stores, such as Home Depot and CompUSA, also have relatively cheap and simple office furniture. And be creative. A hollow-core door from the local lumber store on top of two used Steelcase file cabinets is a first-rate starter desk. Total cost: about $150.

DESK AND TABLES

Start with a minimum of two surfaces, one for your paperwork and projects, another for your computer and printer. The best office setup is a U-shaped or L-shaped arrangement, so when you spin around in your rolling chair all your needs will be within arm's reach. The ideal writing desk is 28 to 30 inches high. Your computer desk should be 26 inches high, allowing your elbows to remain at right angles while you type. If you already have a desk for your computer that is higher, you can customize it by adding a keyboard tray that slides out underneath. As a rule, your keyboard surface should be one to two inches above your knees.

DESK CHAIR

Even if you've been making do with a kitchen stool, trust us, once you're working at full tilt you'll be grateful for a supportive seat. A bad chair with thin cushioning and a rigid backrest will cut into your productivity and creative flow (not to mention your blood flow)—and plain old put you in a crabby mood. The key is adjustability: you want a chair that can accommodate different tasks from typing, to drafting reports, to daydreaming. The best chair should have a contoured cushion seat, a five pronged rolling wheel base, a height adjustment, arms that you can rest your weary limbs on from time to time, and a sturdy back that can be moved forward and back. Some of the high-quality office outfitters like Steelcase and Herman Miller have home-office lines at affordable prices. Steelcase's Turnstone collection is available through Steelcase dealers, and Herman Miller for the Home is available at home-office stores.

LIGHTING

Eyestrain from poor lighting can cause headaches and irritability, both of which will severely cramp your work style. If you'll be spending hours at your computer or bent over documents, plan for plenty of light. There are two kinds of lighting to consider when setting up your office: ambient and task light. The best ambient light is daylight. But even if you work in a sunny office, you'll want added wattage for late-night cram sessions and cloudy days. For ambient light, opt for overheard fixtures—track lights, which can be adjusted, are best, but hanging or floor lamps are fine too. Then to spotlight your tasks, look for desk lamps that use three-way incandescent or halogen bulbs that take up to 100 or 150 watts. Tip: If you spend a lot of time at the computer, make sure your ambient light is not brighter than your computer screen.

Figure that you need about 2 watts per square foot of space. If you have a 12-by-12 office space, count on at least three 100-watt bulbs (144 square feet × 2 = 288 watts). Get bulbs that burn bright. Most cost effective are fluoroscents for your overhead fixtures. But since their light can make you feel like you're in a depressing chain drugstore, buy the warm white variety, which are less brash. Tip: 18 watts of fluorescent light equal 75 watts of incandescent light. For your task lamps, choose incandescent or halogen bulbs, which are easier on the eyes. If your room lacks sunlight or you're prone to seasonal affective disorder, full-spectrum bulbs, which mimic sunlight, are worth the premium price. They produce a warm, pink glow that will keep your spirits high on darker days or during an all-night panic session. And keep your color scheme monochromatic. Aching eyes result in part from looking from bright to dark colors—like from a light screen to a black desk.

STORAGE SPACE

Clutter can be distracting and make you feel (and look) out of control. Invest in good shelving and cabinets to store papers, books, and projects. If you can afford to have custom-made shelves, you'll appreciate the space-saving design. But you can easily buy cheap ready-made shelves from an office supply store or an unfinished cabinet store. If you tend to be messy, the more organizational devices the better.

Stick with sturdy file cabinets made from reinforced steel with double-hung drawers. They're pricey, but the cheaper ones will quickly buckle under heavy loads and slow down your day (and eventually break down altogether). Luckily you can find high-quality file cabinets at used-furniture stores or auctions.

Invest in Time-Saving Equipment

Thanks to the microchip, you can outfit your office with compact, high-powered equipment that will pack the punch of a payroll of twenty. A good answering service can serve as your receptionist, a well-equipped PC can turn out letter-perfect documents, and an E-mail address can connect you to the world. Who needs a staff when you have technology? What's more, thanks to price wars and technological advances, you can get twice as much machinery for about half the cost as you could just five years ago.

Technology is enticing, but resist the urge to overbuy. You can always add a fax machine or trade up to a larger monitor when business and cash flow pick up. Think carefully about what your needs will be, since some pieces have multiple functions. For instance, most PCs can handle incoming faxes and serve as your answering machine as well. We've assembled an inventory of the basic items you'll need to get started (see the box on page 94 for Shopping Tips). Here's a rundown on what to consider:

COMPUTER

Most first-time buyers are tempted to buy the biggest and most powerful machine they can afford. After all, they're told, the technology is changing so fast that what you purchase today will be obsolete in two years. Don't buy it. Decide what your business needs are first, then find a machine that fits your requirements. If you're just setting up business, ask others in your field what machine they chose, what software they use, and any regrets they have about their purchases. If the process seems daunting, then hire a consultant for an hour to help you narrow down your options. Ask colleagues for recommendations. Spending $100 to $200 on expert advice up front could save you thousands of dollars and hours of misery down the line.

One of the first debates is whether to buy an IBM compatible that runs Windows (commonly referred to as a PC) or a Macintosh made by Apple. For most people, a PC is best. PCs comprise about 90% of the computers used in home offices, and therefore virtually all the software programs are written in the PC language. Plus, PCs tend to be cheaper, and any peripherals you add, like a scanner, backup drive, or memory, will also be less pricey. Choose a Mac if you have particular graphics needs that only a Mac can handle or if your business computer is doubling as the family PC and your kids are using Macs at school. No matter what, expect to pay about $2,000 to $3,500 for a fully equipped computer.

Here are some basic facts about a computer's anatomy to help you make head-to-head comparisons:

• **Microprocessor.** The microprocessor is the brains of the computer and tells you how quickly the machine will run (the speed is measured in megahertz, MHz). To give you an idea how far we've come, the first IBM machine, introduced in 1981, ran at 8 MHz. Today's zippy Pentiums run at 200MHz. The fancier the chip, the more you'll pay. Start with a minimum of 100MHz, go for more if you're running power-hungry multimedia programs.

• **RAM.** Random access memory (measured in megabytes— MB) tells you how much temporary information your computer can handle at once. The higher the RAM, the bigger the files you can open, the larger the software programs you can run, and the greater the number of applications you can keep open at once. Windows 95, for instance, requires 16 MB. Most database and graphic programs require 16MB too, so don't go any lower unless all you plan to do is write and print letters.

• **Hard drive.** Think of this as your computer's attic space. The hard drive is where all your software programs and document files are permanently stored. The bigger the hard drive, which is measured in megabytes (MB) or gigabytes (one GB equals roughly 1,000 MB), the more programs and files you can store in your computer. Start with the biggest hard drive you can afford—typically twice as much as you may think you'll need. Software programs are getting bigger and bigger, and chances are you'll keep finding more and more uses for your PC. A good starting point would be about 1,000 megabytes, or 1 gigabyte.

• **CD-ROM.** On most new machines a CD-ROM (compact disk-read only memory) drive is standard. CD-ROMs look just like music CDs and store about 650 MB of data, 464 times (!) more than a regular 3^1/$_2$-inch floppy disk. The most common use for CD-ROMs these days is running children's programs and games. But you can also play your regular music CDs on your computer. A nice bonus: You can send out invoices and listen to Bach at the same time. Look for a drive that runs at a speed of at least 8X.

• **Modem.** Many computers come preloaded with a modem—a device that sends and receives computer signals over the phone line. You'll need a modem if you want to use electronic mail and to send and receive faxes via your PC. Make sure you buy a fast one, 28.8 bps minimum, otherwise you could wait 10 minutes or more to get on-line. Slower modems are cheaper to buy but may cost you more in the long run in phone-line charges.

• **Tape back-up system.** If you plan on storing large files, like a database, financial spreadsheets, or 100-page proposals, buy a backup system. Each night you can back up your entire hard drive on the tape cartridge and then stow it in your company safe. If your PC is stolen, or your hard drive crashes, you won't have to close down shop.

• **Printer.** You have three basic choices: dot matrix, ink jet, or laser. Dot matrix machines are the cheapest, but are noisy and produce amateurish documents. Since ink jets and lasers have fallen dramatically in price, you're better off spending a few extra bucks for the better quality.

An ink jet creates images by spraying ink from nozzles directly onto paper. Ink-jet images are fine for invoices and simple word-processed documents. But if you need clear, crisp printouts for presentations and you print a lot, then go for a laser printer. They use a light beam to transfer images to paper and so can print an entire sheet at a time. Because laser printers are faster, and their cartridges are cheaper, they are actually more cost efficient to run. The only caveat is if you plan to print in color. Ink-jet quality is higher for color printing than lasers.

FAX MACHINE

What did we ever do before fax machines? If you need to send documents frequently and fast, a fax is a great alternative to costly overnight mail or messenger services. If you have a fax modem in your PC, you can fax straight from your computer to a fax machine or another computer and you can also receive faxed documents right into your PC. This route makes sense if all you fax is PC-generated documents, like invoices or reports.

But if you have broader faxing needs, like faxing forms or magazine articles, then invest in a stand-alone machine. We recommend the plain-paper models. The old-fashioned thermal machines are cheaper, but they use special slick paper that winds into a frustrating curl after printing, and the faxed images fade with time. Some features to look for when you buy: a copy option that lets you use your fax machine to make copies, memory that keeps long documents in storage in case your paper runs out, a large (200 sheets or more) paper tray—a must if you tend to receive large faxes or are away from the office for long stretches, and a line-sharing device so you can put your fax, phone, and answering machine on the same line.

COPIER

If your fax machine won't cover your copy needs, splurge on a basic copier. As with all office equipment, the more you spend, the more features you'll get. If space counts, get a machine that does not have a moving platten (the piece that moves back and forth to make the copy), which needs twice as much width as a stationary copier. Settle for no less than a copy rate of 12 sheets per minute, and consider whether you want an extra perk like a legal tray or a extralarge paper tray. When shopping, make sure the price includes a toner cartridge, which when bought alone can cost a hefty $70 or so.

MULTI-COPY DEVICE

Technology is astounding. Now you can buy a combination printer, fax, and copier in one compact unit. If you don't own any equipment yet, buying a multipurpose machine may be a smart move. They cost less than half what you would pay if you bought all those pieces separately. Some pricey models even include a scanner. But you might not get all the features you want in one machine, so check out the offerings carefully. Then think about the ramifications if your multipurpose machine goes kaput. Would your entire operation be brought to a halt? If so, you might be better off with individual devices.

ANSWERING SERVICE

The first contact your customers have with you and your business may be your answering machine. So pick a professional system. These days there are a multitude of choices that fall roughly into three categories: an old-fashioned answering machine, an answering service, and your trusty PC. If you don't receive many calls each day, a machine, either tape or digital, is the most cost effective route. Machines have the advantage of letting you screen calls in the office. A service, which you can get through your local phone company, costs about $6 to $20 a month, and will take messages while you are on the phone (much better than pesty call waiting). Both answering machines and voice-mail systems now let you set up separate mailboxes, a good option to consider if you have employees. If you're a PC whiz, you might investigate software that lets your computer log in and record your messages. Many programs offer nifty features like multiple mailboxes and the ability to retrieve both phone messages and faxes while you're on the road.

ON-LINE SERVICE

Every home business owner needs to have access to the information superhighway. The Internet lets you communicate cheaply with clients and colleagues via electronic mail (E-mail) and have access to numerous forums and Web sites. The question is: What's the best way to get on-line? You can join one of the three major services—CompuServe, America Online, or Prodigy—or you can sign up with a local Internet provider. The large providers offer more services, such as member forums. CompuServe, for instance, has the Working From Home Forum (GO WORK), and America Online has the Small Office Home Office (SOHO) and Small Business Resource Center (YOUR BUSINESS) sites. But if you're more interested in surfing the Net and plan on spending more than ten hours on-line a month, then it makes more financial sense to join an Internet service that will charge a higher monthly fee but will allow you unlimited on-line time.

CELL PHONES AND PAGERS

Need to be in contact with your clients at all times? Then invest in a cellular phone or a pager. You can then give immediate response to a customer query, before he or she gets disgruntled and calls on another expert.

Pagers, those pocket-sized gizmos that receive short messages via radio and satellite signals, are the simplest way to stay in touch, and they now come with a dizzying array of features. The basic models display the number of the person who is trying to reach you. Newer models send full-text messages like "We got the deal, please call me ASAP," and some will even let you respond with your own text answer. Kathy Tompkins, a realtor in Olney, Maryland, never leaves home without her pager. Even when she goes to her kids' softball games or out shopping, she brings her beeper. That way she can slip off to make a call when an important message comes in.

Cell phones are more costly to operate than pagers, because you must pay for incoming as well as outgoing calls. But if you will be far from phones, say showing houses in a new development or installing PCs in an empty office building, a portable phone makes good business sense.

SHOPPING TIPS

For the best deals on computers, look first at office and computer superstores such as CompUSA, Office Depot, or Staples. Mail order is another good source. Because you are buying direct from the manufacturer you'll get a price break, plus you won't have to pay sales tax, which could amount to a couple hundred dollars or more on a $3,000 unit. Gateway (800-846-2000) and Dell (800-879-3355) both make excellent computer systems at good prices.

Another option: computer shows. These traveling malls feature hundreds of PC dealers that offer rock-bottom prices on everything from faxes to phones to the latest computers. You can cut deals at 20% to 40% lower than retail prices. But you have to know your bits from your bytes to get a good deal. If you're not a computer whiz, bring someone who is. Kimberly Stansell, editor and publisher of the newsletter *Bootstrappin' Entrepreneur*, bought a PC clone at a show in Orange County in 1991 for $1,800, about 40% less than the going rate. Stansell brought along a computer consultant friend, who had shopped expos before, to help her out. Her computer-savvy pal was able to haggle over prices and make sure she was getting high-grade components. Five years later, her PC clone is still humming. Look in the business section of your local paper for show listings.

If cash is tight, and you're not sure exactly what your business needs will be in six months, consider leasing. Superstores and specialty office-equipment outlets usually lease basic equipment for one to five years. The longer the lease, the smaller your payment—so go for the longest you can afford. But be forewarned that without a business track record, retailers may ask you to sign a personal guarantee stating that you'll come up with the cash even if your business goes bye-bye. They'll probably run a personal credit check on you as well.

FOR MORE INFORMATION

• *The Home Business Bible* by David R. Eyler ($17.95; John Wiley & Sons) covers a range of topics from telephone services to time management in an easy-to-read encyclopedia form.

• *The Frugal Entrepreneur* by Terri Lonier ($12.95, Portico Press; 800-222-7656) offers cost-saving tips for soloists.

• *Home Office Computing* magazine has frequent articles on home office design, software, hardware, and office equipment ($19.97/year; 800-544-2917).

Insure Your Business

Don't forget insurance. Even if your office consists of a PC, a desk, and a secondhand chair, you'll want coverage in case of a minor catastrophe. A power surge, for instance, could burn out your computer and all the files on it, putting you out of business for days or weeks. Your homeowner's policy may or may not cover your business. Even if it does, the coverage will be nominal—typically up to $2,500 for equipment and $250 for damage that occurs to goods you take out of your home.

How much insurance do you need? Well, that depends on the type of business you operate. You'll definitely want to have all your equipment covered in case of fire or theft. But do you also have a cell phone, pager, or laptop that you take out on the road? Then you'll want off-premises coverage, too. How about liability? Even if the only person who comes to your office is the FedEx deliverer, you'll need coverage in case he or she slips on your icy porch and wants to sue. What would happen if all your equipment got fried by a lightning bolt and you couldn't work for two weeks? Many policies offer what's known as business interruption insurance. Luckily, most insurers have wised up to the growth of home-based businesses and offer policies tailor-made for your needs. Your options fall into three broad categories:

• **Homeowner's insurance plus rider.** If you have a fairly simple and low-tech business, then all you may need is a rider to extend the benefits of your current policy. For as little as $20 or so you can get extra coverage for your computer and fax machine. But you won't be able to sign up for business liability protection or business interruption insurance. If you need that extra coverage then turn to a combination policy (keep reading).

• **Homeowner's/business owner's combination policy.** The beauty of these bundled plans is that you can avoid gaps or duplication in coverage that might occur if you had both a homeowner's and a business policy. A number of insurers such as CNA are now offering these plans to home-based business owners. CNA's HomeWork offers up to $15,000 of coverage for off-premises property damage, one year of business interruption if equipment failure causes you to shut down, and $10,000 of accounts-receivable coverage—for $175 a year. The catch: You also have to have your homeowner's policy with CNA. Combo policies are ideal for home-office-based businesses like management consultants or psychologists. However, if your business is more complicated—say you're operating a day-care center, have employees, or are running a catering business from your home—then you'll need to consider a business insurance policy.

• **Business insurance policy.** These stand-alone policies can be tailor-made for your specific needs. Certain states mandate that home-based businesses must have separate coverage apart from their homeowner's policy. You can either buy a few different policies from several insurers or look for one company to cover all your needs. A comprehensive business package can offer everything from equipment coverage to income insurance to general liability.

To make sure you get adequate coverage, look for an insurance agent or broker who understands your business. Ask colleagues with similar businesses or the local chapter of your professional association for referrals. If you come up dry, call the Independent Insurance Agents of America (800-221-7917). A good agent will help you think through every possible risk you face. One warning: Don't fudge on the scope of your business to get lower rates. It will only backfire when the time comes to make a claim.

Next, compare quotes with similar policies from two or three big outfits like Geico, State Farm, and Allstate. The Home Business Institute (888-DIALHBI) and SOHOA (888-764-6211) also offer business insurance policies to members.

FOR MORE INFORMATION

• *The National Insurance Consumer Helpline* (800-942-4242) will answer basic insurance questions and refer you to agencies for further help. Request their free brochures, *Insuring Your Home Business* and *Insuring Your Business Against a Catastrophe.*

Insure Yourself

Protecting your company makes good business sense. Protecting your well-being does, too. Fall ill or become disabled and you'll not only suffer a loss of income, but your entire business could go down the tubes. Now that you're blissfully on your own, you have the not-so-blissful chore of finding your own insurance coverage—not fun. Individual policies are notoriously expensive, and good group policies are hard to find. The key to finding the best coverage at the right price? Research, research, research. Figure out what your insurance needs are and then look for the policy that will give you the greatest coverage. Tip: Don't try to insure for every possible vagary that could befall you. Instead, focus on the situations that could put you out of commission and totally drain your resources. Here's a rundown on how to find proper health, life, and disability coverage:

HEALTH INSURANCE

Put down on paper a list of the medical expenses you expect for the coming year. Then consider any special conditions that may require a specific doctor or treatment program. Last, how wedded are you (and your family) to your doctors? How would your three-year-old react to a new pediatrician? Or you or your spouse to a different general practitioner? Good news, though: Thanks to the 1996 Health Insurance Portability and Accountability Act, you can deduct a greater portion of your premiums, up to 80% by the year 2006, up from just 40% in 1997.

Managed care vs. Fee-for-service. Your first consideration will be whether you want to be in a managed-care plan—a plan that controls costs by offering a preselected network of physicians—or an old-fashioned fee-for-service plan. In general, it makes most financial sense to be in managed care, which fall into two main categories: HMOs (health maintenance organizations) and PPOs (preferred provider organizations). Annual premiums could be higher (the average HMO family premium is about $6,000 a year), but your annual outlay will be lower since office visits cost only $5 to $15. And managed-care plans offer a range of free or low-cost preventive services such as mammograms, annual checkups, and immunizations. But the savings come at a cost. You'll be limited to a set menu of doctors and you may not be able to have any medical procedure you want, when you want. The most restrictive plans are HMOs. So if choice is important, a PPO makes more sense. These hybrid plans offer the option of seeing a low-cost network doctor for a low co-pay, or straying outside the network and receiving a reimbursement for 50% to 80% of the cost. HMOs, on the other hand, generally do not reimburse you at all when you go out of network.

If you intend to see only your own doctors, or anticipate medical procedures that a managed-care plan might question, then opt for fee-for-service (you can always switch to a managed-care plan if the higher fees become prohibitive). Your strategy should be to go for catastrophic coverage with a high deductible and low premiums. You want coverage for the costs that could totally wipe you out, say if you end up in intensive care or need costly chemo treatments, not for minor exams that you could afford to pay for out of pocket. Look for a policy that has an out-of-pocket limit of $2,500 and then keep at least that much in an emergency fund. If a disaster does occur and you hit the limit, your insurer will then pay at 100%. The policy should cover basic hospital stays and have an annual payout of at least $500,000, though $1 million is better. To augment your catastrophic coverage, sign up for the newly established medical savings account (MSA). A provision of the 1996 Health Insurance Act, the MSA lets you sock away 65% of the cost of your deductible (75% for families) in a tax-deferred account to pay for medical expenses. To qualify for an MSA you must have bought a policy with a deductible of $1,500 to $2,250 as an individual or $3,000 to $4,500 for a family.

Finding the policy. Ask your colleagues for names of insurance brokers they trust. You can also call up the major carriers in your area and give them your requirements and see what they will offer up. By talking directly to an insurer you can often dicker for a better deal. Because groups typically offer the lowest rates, also call up any professional or trade associations you belong to and ask for the specs on their policies. Organizations like SOHOA (888-764-6211), National Association of the Self-Employed (800-232-NASE), and Home Business Institute (888-DIALHBI) have group policies for members and usually offer more than one plan to choose from. Your local chamber of commerce may also have a group policy for members. Last, find out if your state has a group cooperative for small business owners or the self-employed. Call the Institute for Health Policy Solutions (202-857-0810) to find out if there is a coop in your state. Another idea: Wilkinson Benefit Consultants (800-296-3030) will search for the best three carriers for your health needs for a fee of $270.

Don't forget COBRA. If you're just about to leave a full-time job, you may be able to continue on your employer's plan, so long as your company employs more than 20 people. Under the Consolidated Omnibus Reconciliation Act, or COBRA, your employer is required to let you remain on the group's medical plan for up to 18 months. You pay the monthly group-rate premiums, which will most likely be lower than what you'll encounter in the open market. If you find something better, you can always switch out.

LIFE INSURANCE

For starters, you only need life insurance if you have dependents. If you're happily single without kids, you can happily skip this section. How much coverage do you need? Simply put, if you are the sole breadwinner, you need to leave enough money when combined with your other assets, to provide a lifetime income stream for your family. And if you have college-bound kids, your benefit should also help fund their college accounts. Lew Altfest, a New York City fee-only certified financial planner, offers this formula: Four times your income for your spouse plus two times for each child. Then subtract your investment assets and your anticipated Social Security payout (call 800-772-1213 to get a free earnings and benefits estimate). Presto. You have your benefit. Use this number as a rough guide and then talk to a trustworthy financial planner to fine-tune it. Unless you're a high-wheeling investor, avoid complicated cash-value policies and opt for a simple term policy.

Look for a policy that is guaranteed renewable and non-cancelable, and high quality. A life insurer with financial problems may suddenly raise your rates, or worse yet, go out of business. Choose one that is rated AA or better. Again, compare rates among various insurers and contact all your professional organizations to find out their group rates. A couple of insurers to check out: USAA Life (800-531-8000) and Ameritas Life Insurance Company (800-552-3553). Another option is a free shopping service. One of the biggest, QuoteSmith (800-431-1147; Quotesmith.com) has a database of about 140 carriers. If you're still employed and in a high-risk category (a recent heart attack or high cholesterol could do it), ask if you can pay your own premium and stay on your soon to be ex-employer's plan. If they let you, you'll most likely get a better rate than you'd find on your own.

DISABILITY INSURANCE

Most of us are more comfortable thinking about death than disability. But the reality is that your odds of being disabled at some point in your career are six times greater than your chances of dying. Even Superman (aka Christopher Reeve) got felled. So proper coverage is important, especially when you're self-employed and your business is at stake. You might be thinking, "Oh, Social Security will cover me." Social Security only kicks in when you're completely disabled and can't work at all (translation: You're practically wheelchair bound).

You need a policy that covers 60% of your income until you reach age 65. Since you'll be paying the premiums with taxable dollars and won't have to pay taxes on the benefit payments, that amount should practically replace your income. Like your life insurance policy, your disability coverage should also be renewable and noncancelable. Also important is a policy that has an "own occupation" clause, meaning that you'll be covered as long as you cannot do your current job. Without such a clause your insurer might cut you off, insisting that you could work quite well as, say, a cashier.

Disability insurance can be mighty hard to come by when you're self-employed. The insurer's quandary is: How do you prove that someone who works at home is actually disabled? Investigate all avenues to find good coverage, including all the professional groups you belong to. Also, if you have a financial planner, ask him or her to help out. Jeff Wuorio, a freelance writer in Maine, was turned down by the carrier who provided his homeowner's and auto insurance policies and two other insurers—even though he was in tiptop health. Finally, he went to his planner, who used his long-standing relationship with an insurance agent to get Wuorio a guaranteed renewable and noncancelable long-term disability policy.

Insure Your Future with a Simple Retirement Plan

We know. The last place you want to put your money right now is in a retirement account. You're probably more worried about cash flow than having a cash cow at age 65. You might even think, "What, me, retire?" But the day may come when you'd rather be lobbing tennis balls in Miami than logging numbers into your P&L statement. Plus, with the future of Social Security on the skids and your life expectancy ratcheting up year after year, you'll need a cushion, no matter how optimistic your plans are for your business. So it's best to get started, even with small contributions, ASAP. Know why? The beauty of compounding. Say you put just $2,500 away each year from age 30 to age 65, and it grows at 8% a year. You'd have a total of $430,000 after 35 years. If you waited till you were 45 to start saving, you'd have to sock away $5,880 a year to reach that same lofty amount in 20 years' time.

Now, where to put the cash? You have two good choices: a SEP-IRA (Simplified Employee Pension-Individual Retirement Account), or a Keogh. You can set both plans up at a bank, mutual fund company, or brokerage and direct your savings to any investment vehicle you want. Both plans are appropriate whether you are a sole proprietorship, S corp, or limited partnership. If your savings needs are basic, we recommend SEPs. Like the name implies, SEPs are simple to set up and administer. To start the account you fill out a one-page form and file it with the trustee you have chosen. Under a SEP you can stash 13% of your adjusted net business profit or $22,500, whichever is less. And the beauty of a SEP is that you don't have to set up the account until tax time.

If business is booming, a Keogh will let you put away 20% of your adjusted net profits or $30,000—again, whichever is less. But to reach that 20% goal you must set up two separate plans, a profit-sharing plan and a money purchase plan (although some brokerage firms will allow you to combine the two). The profit-sharing works like a SEP, and you can contribute up to 13% of your net earnings to it. For more bang, you can add a money purchase plan and contribute enough to bring you to the 20% cap. But the money purchase plan has to be funded each year at the same rate. You can't flake out on your contributions one year if you've had bad profits. With a Keogh, you must set up your plan by December 31, though you still have until April 15 to make your contributions.

Confused? Call a financial planner. An experienced planner can help you determine how much money you'll need in retirement, how much you should be socking away each year, and what plan makes the most sense. If you're the independent type, you can also buy a software package like Quicken Financial Planner or Vanguard Retirement Planner (DOS or Windows; 800-950-1971) to figure out your future financial needs.

FOR MORE INFORMATION

• *The* MONEY *Book of Personal Finance* by Richard Eisenberg explains how to choose health-insurance and retirement plans in basic terms ($24.95; Warner Books).

TAKING CARE OF YOUR 401(K)

Ah, the difficulties of cutting loose. Among the decisions you'll have to face: figuring out what to do with your 401(k) account. You may be tempted to spend your entire cache on a Pentium PC and a color laser printer. Or you may just let the money sit around while you tend to more pressing matters, like designing your company's new logo. Neither move is wise.

Don't spend the money. Unless you're years from retirement or strapped for start-up cash, don't touch the balance. By withdrawing from your account before age 59½ you could lose more than 50% to Uncle Sam. You'll have to pay a nasty 10% early withdrawal penalty, plus income taxes. If you wait until you retire to use the money, you won't take so much of a sting since your tax rate will be lower. And chew on this: You can always find a way to scare up money for your business— whether you have to beg or borrow—but who will lend you money to live on in retirement?

Roll the 401(k) into an IRA. Even if your company will let you keep your 401(k) account, it's usually smarter to start your own IRA. That way you can invest the money any way you want, rather than face the restrictions of your 401(k)'s offerings. Just like with a SEP or Keogh, you can open your IRA at a bank, brokerage house, or mutual fund—depending on your investing taste. Once you know where you want the money to go, arrange for a trustee-to-trustee transfer into what's known as a conduit IRA. You should keep your 401(k) money separate from your other retirement accounts. Should you decide to rejoin the corporate world, you'll still have the option to roll your 401(k) back into your new employer's plan. You can't do that if you have mixed the funds with other non-401(k) money.

Take risks. Your instinct may be to play it safe with your retirement money. After all, you may be gambling with every other asset you have. Still, your best returns will come from placing the majority of your account in stocks, which historically yield nearly twice as much as bonds over long stretches of time. And if your savings are substantial—say over $10,000—diversify. Allocate your money between different kinds of investments. If for instance, you're a mutual fund investor, open large and small cap stock funds, an international fund, and perhaps put a small portion, say 10% to 20%, in bonds.

CHAPTER 5

Tax Smarts for the Home Business

If your eyes instantly glaze over at the mention of taxes, get yourself a strong cup of java. You won't want to doze through this chapter. As you'll find out, failure to keep careful business records and deduct your expenses the right way could cost you your business and lead you straight to bankruptcy court. The fact is, when you go solo, you take on far more demanding responsibilities as a taxpayer. Only the self-employed, for instance, face the slippery task of projecting all of the money they'll earn in a year. And with no employer deducting taxes regularly, soloists have to file payments on those estimated earnings each quarter. What's more, they owe a wounding 100% of Medicare and Social Security taxes, since no employer is there to pick up half the tab.

All this may sound pretty grim. But before you abandon your dream of working at home, here's the good news: As a business owner, you're eligible for a slew of deductions that salaried employees don't get. Even better, when you run your business out of your home, you can write off everything from a portion of your gas bill to your carpet cleaner's visit. And

107

believe us, you'll need to take advantage of every deduction you can in order to make up for benefits you lost when you left your corporate job, such as a health plan. While we don't expect to turn you into a tax pro, we'll make you aware of your tax rights as a business owner. In this chapter, we'll walk you through:

- How to structure your company
- Business write-offs you can claim
- Criteria for taking a home-office deduction
- Tips for keeping audit-proof records
- Recouping your start-up costs
- Finding a tax pro

Choosing Your Business MO

Before you make your first sale, you need to choose a business structure within which to operate. This may sound like yet another tedious task on your to-do list, but in reality, it's one of the most important planning moves you'll make. The business form you take affects the type of paperwork you must file with state and local authorities, the tax forms you must fill out and the deductions you can take, the personal liability protection you'll receive, and even the amount of money you can set aside for retirement. That's good reason to read this section over carefully—and then consult a tax pro if necessary. An accountant can crunch numbers in a variety of ways to find out which setup would best suit your situation. (For help picking a CPA, see our box in this chapter.)

We'll help you research your options by providing a helpful primer on different business forms. In general, if you're going into business by yourself, you have two options: a sole proprietorship or a corporation. If you're going into business with another person, you can choose between a partnership, a corporation, and a limited liability company. Here's a rundown on your options:

SOLE PROPRIETORSHIP

Most entrepreneurs opt for a sole proprietorship because it's by far the easiest to start. You simply fill out a few forms required by your municipality or state such as a business license or occupancy permit. You'll also need to file a DBA, which stands for "doing business as," so that no one else can use your company's name.

Advantages. You don't need the assistance of an attorney or an accountant to get started. You simply attach a Schedule C form to your personal return, or 1040, listing business income and expenses. Then the net profit of the business is added to your 1040 and taxed at your personal rate—from 15% to 39.6%. "I opted for a sole proprietorship for its simplicity," says Loren Steen, who runs a home-based seafood brokerage. "The less paperwork, the better."

Disadvantages. You're liable for business debts as if you had incurred them as personal debts. If a customer gets food poisoning from your catering business, that customer could sue for damages, going after your business assets, as well as your life savings and even your house. Another disadvantage of sole proprietorships is that they don't extend beyond your lifetime. If you want to pass your business to your children, you may need to incorporate.

PARTNERSHIP

If you plan on working with another person, you may opt for a partnership. As with a sole proprietorship, you don't need to file any formal papers. But tread carefully here. Although you don't need a written agreement, it's a wise idea to draw up a contract detailing each partner's investment and responsibilities in the business. The business is reported on its own tax return (Form 1065), but it doesn't pay corporate taxes. Instead, income or losses are tallied and then each partner files a separate return, using a Schedule K-1, that includes the amount of his or her tax liability based on each partner's profit-sharing split.

Advantages. It allows you a fairly straightforward way to go into business with another person. And by having a co-worker, you double your efforts and resources.

Disadvantages. You're responsible not only for your own liabilities but for those of your partner as well. If your partner doesn't pay a company bill, you may have to spot him or her. What's more, you will have to agree with your partner on such issues as retirement plans, since only one type is allowed.

LIMITED PARTNERSHIP

This business structure is similar to that of a general partnership, except that one partner plays an active role in running the business, while the other, limited partner is typically a "passive" investor who has no say in the management of the business. As such, the limited partner's liability is restricted to the amount of his or her investment in the company. This allows the limited partner to share profits without being exposed to large business debts.

Advantages. A limited partnership provides a way for you to raise capital by including another investor.

Disadvantages. You'll face greater filing requirements, which vary with each state, due to the special protection extended to the limited partner. Plus, if the business incurs any debts, as the active partner, you have complete liability.

FINDING A TOP-NOTCH TAX ADVISOR

If you find IRS publications more arcane than an ancient Greek manuscript, don't be shy about seeking a translator. The money you'll spend on a tax pro will save you endless hours of frustration—and perhaps a costly error or two that you would have made on your own. Even if you're a whiz at filing your own taxes, you may want to turn to a CPA or an enrolled agent for help determining which business structure is best for you. Here are some tips on how to go about finding an expert:

•**Seek recommendations** from trusted friends who are in business or from professionals such as bankers whose judgment you respect.

•**Interview three or four tax advisors** before selecting one. Find out what they specialize in—and don't go with a jack of all trades. Tax law is so complicated that you need someone who handles a lot of clients with a business structure similar to yours.

•**Ask for references.** Get the names of business owners who have been clients for at least three years. Ask them how satisfied they are with the service they've received.

•**Check credentials.** Consider hiring a CPA or an enrolled agent—both of whom have had to pass harrowing examinations to earn their designation. What's more, in the unlucky scenario that you're audited, most CPAs and enrolled agents will represent you (an H&R Block preparer, on the other hand, won't represent you—unless he or she is an enrolled agent). If you ever have to litigate a claim in court, however, your best bet is to go with a lawyer. Any tax pro except a lawyer can be subpoenaed to testify against you.

•**Avoid a one-person shop.** Larger firms usually have one pro prepare the return and another look it over for errors. One small typo could cost you hundreds of dollars and even trigger an audit. So going with a firm of two or three CPAs will provide you with better protection.

C CORPORATION

By incorporating your business, you create an entity that's separate from yourself. As such, you must file a separate corporate return (Form 1120) and pay corporate taxes, in addition to personal income taxes on the wages or dividends you distribute to yourself.

Advantages. As you probably guessed, incorporating does bring many desirable perks. Otherwise business owners wouldn't subject themselves to double taxation. These pluses include:

• **Liability protection.** When you incorporate, you shield your personal assets and those of your family from creditors. In other words, if the corporation incurs debt, creditors can only go after corporate assets. What's more, shareholders aren't personally liable for corporate actions.

Don't be blasé about liability protection. "If you invented a new drug or another type of product that lends itself to litigation, you might want to incorporate," warns Isabelle Levin, a CPA with Goldstein, Golub, Kessler & Company in New York City. Actuarial and computer consultant Christopher Maher incorporated his business in part to save on insurance. "Professional liability insurance for an actuary is very expensive," he explains. "You really can't purchase enough coverage." In fact, it's less expensive for him to pay a tax attorney to review his corporate return every year.

• **Lower audit rate.** The Internal Revenue Service is more likely to go after an unincorporated business than one that's incorporated.

• **Possibly greater ease in raising money.** Corporations can issue stock to the general public to raise money, and they may appear more solid in the eyes of lenders as well.

• **Fringe benefits.** A C corporation can provide greater tax-favored benefits to its employees, such as more generous pension and medical reimbursement plans.

Disadvantages. Corporations are typically more expensive to start, more highly regulated, and may force you to seek the assistance of an accountant to help you with regular record keeping.

For instance, you must file articles of incorporation, create corporate bylaws, and fill other state requirements. You also have to issue stock, even if you're the sole shareholder. The most significant drawback, of course, is that C corporations pay corporate income tax.

However, if you're in a high personal-income-tax bracket *and* you want your business to grow rapidly, you should consider incorporating. For instance, let's say that you're in the top tax rate for individuals of 39.6%. That's nearly 5 percentage points higher than the steepest corporate rate of 35%. If you don't need your business income to live on, you can re-invest your company's earnings to finance growth. That way you pay 35% of your revenues to Uncle Sam rather than 39.6%.

SUBCHAPTER S CORPORATION

This business form gives you the protection of a corporation and the tax aspects of a partnership or sole proprietorship.

Advantages. There's no liability beyond the assets of the corporation. That's one reason Cory Johnson sought S-corporation status for his Container Alternatives business. "I wanted the full-blown protection of a corporation," says Johnson, whose company manufactures a ready-to-mix powder for making planters, statues, and ornaments for gardens. What's more, while you must file a corporate tax return (in this case, a Form 1120-S), income is generally passed through to the owners and shareholders with no corporate taxes due.

Disadvantages. It's expensive to set up and maintain, and you face more limitations than you would with a partnership or limited liability company. For instance, you can have no more than 75 shareholders, and all of them must be U.S. citizens.

LIMITED LIABILITY COMPANY

This is the newest business structure, and it has become extremely popular. It grants you the limited liability of a corporation with the flexibility and tax status of a partnership. (Note: An LLC requires at least two partners, one of whom can be a spouse.) At press time, only two states—Vermont and Hawaii—had not adopted LLCs.

Advantages. Creating an LLC is much easier and less expensive than creating an S corporation or a C corporation. You simply file "articles of organization" with the appropriate state agency—typically your secretary of state or the cooperation commission. The filing fee is generally less than $100. Unlike an S corporation, you can have an unlimited number of partners. LLCs also have fewer organizational restrictions and reporting requirements than S corporations.

Disadvantages. Some tax pros feel that it's risky to form an LLC, because too few court cases have been handed down regarding this particular business entity. Also, some states bar professional service businesses from operating as LLCs. Check with your accountant or lawyer to see what your state's particular rules are.

FOR MORE INFORMATION

• *Tax Savvy for Small Business* ($26.95; Nolo Press) by tax attorney Frederick Daily provides more detailed information on business forms.

• IRS Publication 334, *Tax Guide for Small Business* (800-829-3676) explains everything from the type of records to keep to how to fill out your tax forms if you're a partnership, sole proprietor, or S corp.

• *What the IRS Doesn't Want You to Know* by Martin Kaplan (1995; Villard Books) offers a convincing argument for the advantages of incorporating.

How to File Self-Employment Tax

Unless you opted to form a subchapter C corporation, you are considered self-employed and owe self-employment taxes. This is one of the more painful realities of going solo. Here's how it works: When you're employed by a company, your employer withholds Social Security and Medicare contributions—called FICA (Federal Insurance Contributions Act) taxes. As an employee, you pay half of your FICA taxes, and your employer pays the rest. But once you're on your own, you're responsible for the whole kit and caboodle. In 1996, the self-employment tax rate of 15.30% applied to net earnings of $62,700 or less, and an additional 2.9% rate applied to net earnings exceeding $62,700. You must compute your liability for self-employment tax using Schedule SE, which you attach to your 1040. Fortunately, you can claim a deduction for half of the amount you pay on Line 25 of your 1040.

As if paying full FICA taxes weren't enough, you also have to fork over payments on your income each quarter. That's because you no longer have an employer deducting taxes from your pay throughout the year. So get ready to send the IRS a check every April 15, June 15, September 15, and January 15—by filing Form 1040-ES. This is true even if you make as little as $400 a year. The trick to quarterly filing, of course, is knowing how much to pay. In effect, you have to project how much you think you'll earn for the whole year by April 15. And that's not easy! If your payments turn out to be too small or if they're not made on time, the IRS will assess an underpayment penalty. To avoid such fees, entrepreneurs with adjusted gross incomes under $150,000 need to pay 100% of last year's tax bill or 90% of this year's liability, whichever is lower. If you make more than $150,000, you need to pay 110% of last year's tab.

FOR MORE INFORMATION

• IRS Publication 505, *Withholding and Estimated Taxes*.

Claiming Your Expenses

Thank goodness you have the chance to make up for those hefty self-employment taxes by writing off a huge range of expenses. In a nutshell, you're entitled to two categories of ongoing deductions: home-office expenses and ordinary business expenses. You can also claim one-time costs you incurred before actually going into business. Called start-up costs, these expenses fall into a category of their own.

RECOUPING YOUR START-UP COSTS

As you've gone about setting up your business, no doubt you've accumulated a tower of bills rivaling Mount Kilimanjaro. There was the costly direct-mail survey you administered to make sure your idea was on track, the zippy Pentium PC you needed to handle everything from billing to answering the phone, and let's not forget the sleek rosewood desk you caved into buying. If you're thinking, "Oh well, at least I can write off those expenses right away," we have some sobering news for you. The IRS won't allow you to deduct expenses in the current tax year that you incurred *before beginning business*. Instead, you must file an election to amortize these expenses over a period of 60 months (IRS Form 4562, Depreciation and Amortization).

For instance, let's say you spent $6,000 conducting market research, buying office supplies and equipment, and printing brochures. Then, four months later, on May 1, you opened for business. All of your expenses prior to May 1 would be considered capital expenditures and are deductible at the rate of $100 a month over the first 60 months you're in business ($6,000/60 = $100). Costs you incur after May 1, however, are 100% deductible in the current tax year (with the exception of business assets, as we explain later).

You can work around this rule by generating income as quickly as possible. For instance, you could take a few customers right away—even before you buy your new desk or computer. That way you're technically in business even while you're still outfitting your office. Or you may be able to delay paying bills to your suppliers until after you've made a sale or two. Keep in mind, however, that the deductions may mean more to you in future tax years when your business is earning more money that you'll want to offset.

EVERYDAY EXPENSES YOU CAN CLAIM IN THE CURRENT TAX YEAR

Advertising costs
Association dues
Bank fees
Beeper service
Books related to your business
Bookkeeping
Business cards
Cellular phone service
Consultant fees
Courses to improve your skills
On-line service
Paper supplies
Postage
Pens and pencils
Professional fees (CPA, lawyer, etc.)
Publicity expense
Repairs for equipment

Seminars
Telephone expenses pertaining to work
Trade-show fees
Wages paid to employees

HOME OFFICE WRITE-OFFS

Carpet cleaning
Cleaning supplies used in office space
Electrical work
Homeowner's insurance
Housecleaning service
Mortgage interest
Plumbing
Property taxes
Rent
Renter's insurance
Roof repair
Telephone (a portion of your regular phone
    or a separate line)
Trash collection
Utilities

WRITING OFF YOUR HOME OFFICE

Most people would rather clean out the garage than tend to their taxes. But when you see how many deductions you can take by running your business out of your home, you may actually take a little pleasure in sending your return to the IRS. For instance, you can slice hundreds of dollars off your mortgage bill or annual rent. Ever thought you could write off part of the tab for home improvements, utilities, even housecleaning? These are all deductible expenses if your home office meets IRS standards. Of course, that's the hitch. You must satisfy the following criteria in order to take the home-office deduction:

1. **You use your home office regularly and *exclusively* for business.** In other words, you must use your home office on a continuing basis to do nothing but run your company. Keeping computer games on your office computer is a no-no. So is tucking a rollaway in the corner of the office for occasional house guests. The IRS isn't Big Brother, but it's serious about the exclusivity test. Sure, you can run your home office out of your dining room—as long as you never have family meals there too. You can even use a corner of your child's playroom as your home office (a perfectly mad idea!), as long as it's a separately identifiable space used for nothing but business. There's one exception to the exclusivity test. If you operate a licensed daycare facility in your living room for children, the elderly, or handicapped persons, you can deduct the use of the room, even if you use it after hours to watch television or entertain friends.

Next, you need to prove that you use your home office regularly. For instance, you may hold meetings with clients every few months in a spare room. Even if you use the room only for those meetings, you can't deduct the space. The IRS would define your use of the room as merely incidental. However, if you use another room on a daily basis exclusively for managing your business, you can deduct expenses for the use of that room. It's a good idea to keep a log of the hours you spend in your office.

You can also deduct space used for inventory, even if it's stored in a room where you stash your luggage or bicycles, as long as the space is separately identifiable. However, your business must be in wholesale or retail sale of products, and, again, you must use the storage space regularly.

2. **You either meet with clients in your home office, or the home office is your principal place of business.** For a home office to qualify as a principal place of business, it must be the site where the most important functions of the business are performed. If it's unclear where the most important business activities take place, then the IRS will consider how much time you spend in your home office. For instance, let's say

you're a painter/carpenter who takes care of paperwork details in a home office but spends most of the day working on people's houses and businesses. In this situation, don't count on a home-office deduction. Similarly, if you're a salesperson who spends hours on the road, forget about taking a home-office deduction. But if you make your sales by phone or mail from the office, deduct away. Unfortunately, millions of home entrepreneurs do most of their income-producing work outside their office, disqualifying them for a home office deduction. However, Congress is considering proposals to allow a deduction for offices that are essentially used for management tasks that can't be performed elsewhere.

Even if your home office isn't your principal place of work, you *can* take the deduction as long as you see clients, customers, or patients regularly at home. Management consultants, financial planners, therapists, and lawyers, for instance, may have an outside office as well as one in the home. The space used to meet with clients is deductible, but the area used for paperwork is not.

An exception: If you locate your office in a freestanding structure on your property such as a detached garage, a workshop, or a barn, you can claim the deduction, even if you don't meet with clients in your office or use it as your principal place of work. You simply have to use the building regularly and exclusively for your business—even if all you do in your office is file papers.

Here's how you calculate your deduction: First take the square footage of your home office, then divide it by your home's total square footage. For instance, let's say you have a 2,000-square-foot home and your home office occupies 200 square feet in the basement rec-room. Ten percent of your home is allocated for business (200/2,000 = 10%). That means that you can deduct 10% of your utilities, housecleaning services, and annual rent. If you're a homeowner, you can deduct part of your mortgage interest and property taxes. (For more deductible home-office expenses, see the list in this chapter.) If you run a day-care service, the formula is more complicated. You must take the percentage of your home devoted to your business and multiply it by the percentage of hours out of the year that you spend operating your business [(Square footage of space used regularly for day care/Total square footage of house) × (Hours of operation per year/Total hours in a year or 8,760)].

THE HOBBY RULE

If you don't make a profit in three out of five years, the Internal Revenue Service may begin to suspect that you're just practicing a hobby, not running a business. Of course, with a little planning, you can pass the "three-out-of-five" test—even if you claim a profit of just $5 or $10 one year. But even businesses that experience losses year after year still qualify for their deductions, as long as they run a professional shop. Having a separate checking account and telephone line, keeping good records, and printing business stationery and cards, for instance, will help your business look less like a pastime and more like a profit-seeking enterprise.

To write off a home office, sole proprietors must attach Form 8829 to their Schedule C form. If you have an incorporated business, you don't have to file a separate form. But you still calculate your deduction in the same manner.

Warning: Don't take a home office deduction the year before you plan to sell your house. If you take the deduction and then sell your house for a profit, you'll owe capital gains taxes on the portion of your house that was used as a home office. That's because the IRS allows you to defer any gains on a home sale as long as the proceeds are plowed into another home. Or, people 55 and older can take a one-time capital gain exclusion on a home sale of up to $125,000. But if you have a home office, a portion of your house is considered business property separate from the residence.

For instance, if you bought your house for $100,000 and sold it for $120,000, you'd have a $20,000 gain. If you had been using 20% of your house as office space, then you'd owe taxes on $4,000 of the gain ($20,000 × 20% = $4,000). Since capital gains are taxed at 28%, you'd owe the IRS a whopping $1,120 (28% × $4,000 = $1,120). To avoid the problem, you can continue using your home office during the year before you sell your house. But don't plan on deducting your home office expenses.

DEDUCTING ORDINARY AND NECESSARY BUSINESS EXPENSES

Even if you don't qualify for a home-office deduction, you can still claim ordinary business expenses, which any business owner—whether he or she works at home or not—can take. Here are the major categories:

• **Auto expenses.** There are two ways to claim vehicle expenses: the mileage method and the actual expense method. If you opt for the mileage method, you simply have to keep track of how many miles you drive for business during the year. (In case you're ever audited, you should keep a log book, recording when the trip took place, where you went, what the business purpose was, and how many miles you drove.) Then you can deduct a set amount—currently 31 cents—for every mile you drive. This figure is supposed to cover gas, repairs, and even insurance.

If you have a new car, you may come out ahead if you use the actual expense method. You'll have to keep track of each individual operating expense (gas, tolls, etc.), but when you use this method, you're also allowed to take a depreciation deduction. We'll explain how that works under "business assets."

• **Bad debt.** Unfortunately, at some point, most businesses get stiffed. If you have a service business, you're out of luck. To keep unscrupulous entrepreneurs from inflating their bills and claiming a lot of bad debt, the IRS doesn't allow any service-oriented business to write off money that clients refuse to pay. Like Millie Szerman, who launched a home-based PR business, your only recourse is to take your deadbeat client to small claims court. If your business provides goods and keeps an inventory, however, you can deduct the cost of the goods not paid for.

• **Business assets.** The IRS, as you know by now, doesn't make anything easy. It considers expenditures for such things as new equipment, inventory, and furniture different from, say, the cost of computer paper and toner cartridges. Since these assets have a useful life beyond the tax year in which you bought them, you must depreciate them. In other words, you have to spread your tax deduction out over a number of years. IRS Publication 534 lists depreciation periods for different assets.

Thanks to Internal Revenue Code 179—one of the few tax codes worth memorizing—you can usually get around depreciating your assets. This rule allows business owners to write off up to $18,000 of business assets as current expenses in 1997. In 1998, the deduction jumps to $18,500, and gradually reaches $25,000 in 2003. Of course, if you have only minimal income from your business right now, you may opt to depreciate your assets to offset future income.

• **Entertainment.** You can deduct 50% of the cost of throwing a party at your house, taking a business contact to lunch, or even hiring a boat for a midnight cruise. But you have to discuss business during the festivities or immediately before or after you entertain clients or employees. You can also make gifts to clients and deduct up to $25 of the cost.

• **Everyday expenditures.** This includes the common items you use in the course of your work: office supplies, postage and shipping, telephone, on-line services, and advertising fees. Some expenses may relate to your particular line of business. If you're a personal chef or a caterer, you could deduct the cost of cookbooks. If you teach computer to kids, you could deduct the cost of software and computer games. If you're a financial planner, you could deduct your subscriptions to *The Wall Street Journal* and MONEY magazine. (See the box in this chapter listing more everyday business expenses.)

• **Health insurance.** Sole proprietors, partners, limited-liability-company members, and S-corporation shareholders can deduct 40% of the health insurance premiums they pay for themselves and their families in 1997. For tax years beginning in 1998 through 2003, you can deduct 45% of your premium. Then the amount starts to rise, and by 2006, they'll be able to write off 80% of the cost of their premiums. For C corporations, health insurance is a great fringe benefit. Premiums paid for owners and employees are 100% deductible to the corporation and tax-free to the recipients.

• **Travel.** When you take a business trip, you can deduct all of your lodging costs and 50% of your meal expenditures. If you decide to extend your stay for a vacation, you can still write off your round-trip travel costs, as well as any expenses incurred while working. But if the trip is mainly for personal reasons, you can only deduct costs that pertain to your business, not including transportation. The rules are even stricter for international travel. You can deduct your transportation costs only if you spend 75% or more of your time conducting business or are outside of the country for less than one week, excluding the day of departure. That means you could zip over to Rome for five days, attend only one business meeting, and still write off your round-trip airfare. If you linger for seven days to tour the city, however, you can't claim your airfare.

Of course, you don't have to go out of town to travel for business. Whenever you leave home to pick up supplies, meet with clients, or do research, you can deduct the cost of the trip. You need to keep a log of your trips, and don't forget to save every taxi receipt or keep track of your vehicle mileage.

FOR MORE INFORMATION

• IRS Publication 587, *Business Use of Your Home*, contains instructions, examples, and a worksheet for calculating your home office deduction.

• IRS Publications 535, *Business Expenses*; 334, *Tax Guide for Small Business*; 463, *Travel, Entertainment and Gift Expenses*; and 917, *Business Use of a Car.*

Proving You Qualify for Your Deductions

You'd think that once you obtained your business license and printed stationery with your company's logo, you'd be home free. But as a final insult, the IRS may say to you, "Hey, we don't think you're *really* self-employed at all." And that could cause both you *and* your clients a serious migraine. If an auditor determines that your relationship with a client was actually that of an employee, you'll have to refile your taxes. And if you've taken a lot of deductions for your home office, health insurance premiums, and business supplies—write-offs you're not eligible for as an employee—you could wind up owing the IRS a hefty amount. Your client is also liable for back taxes—including half of your Social Security tax—interest, and often significant penalties.

Who is in danger of being misclassified as an employee? The agency is especially suspicious of entrepreneurs who run service-oriented businesses—particularly if they work out of their client's office. For instance, many consultants today spend months on their clients' premises overseeing long-term projects, rather than simply providing advice and letting the client implement it. But such an arrangement may make the entrepreneur look like an employee. Here are some other situations that catch the agency's attention:

• You work primarily on one account or for one customer.
• Your client sets your work hours.
• You receive on-the-job training.
• You use your client's equipment.
• You do your work according to your client's instructions.

RECORD-KEEPING TIPS

The Internal Revenue Service is particularly wary of small businesses. Audit rates of unincorporated businesses earning less than $25,000 recently doubled—from 2.2% in 1993 to 4.4% in 1994. If that's not reason enough to maintain organized records of your expenses and income, just listen to Tom Wotherspoon, an advertising copywriter, whose home business was audited in 1986 and again in 1991. "The agent looked at every page in my mileage log and pointed at random to a trip and asked why I needed to go," he says. Fortunately, Wotherspoon kept a detailed appointment book. "I have a page devoted to each day." he says. The agent also asked to see records for all travel and entertainment expenses. "He scrutinized one in four receipts out of 75 or 100 total," says Wotherspoon.

Whether you opt to keep a ledger or use a sophisticated software program, you should follow Wotherspoon's example by keeping careful tabs on your income and outflow. Here are five commandments never to violate:

Use a separate bank account for business transactions. This was one place where Wotherspoon fell short: He failed to keep separate accounts for business and personal expenses. "In 1991, all my business expenses were written on personal checks," he says. "I needed a better division on paper." Fortunately, the IRS did not penalize him, though the agent strongly suggested that he keep his accounts separate in the future.

Pay for expenses by check or credit card, not cash. Even if you're merely buying a few office supplies, it's a good idea to pay with a corporate credit card or by checks with your business name. IRS agents become suspicious if you have a lot of cash transactions. And let's face it, a canceled check or a credit card statement provides better substantiation of your expenses than merely a receipt for cash would.

Keep receipts and ledger sheets for at least three years. That's just the minimum amount of time you have to keep your records. It's even smarter to keep them forever. If you plan on selling the business one day, a prospective buyer may want to see your records. For equipment expenditures, you need to keep a record of your cost basis until you've fully depreciated

---

the asset. The smartest way to handle your receipts and invoices, says financial planner Alan Cohn, is to attach them to the canceled check or monthly credit card statement. "We file all our expenses by check number," says home-based actuarial and computer consultant Christoper Maher. "It's all up in the attic. I've saved everything since I first started my business."

Don't use a shoebox. You don't need a sophisticated filing system, but a cardboard box crammed with receipts won't cut it. There's just no way you can be as organized as you need to if you're using a shoebox. Instead, try an accordion file or a number of manila folders for each category of expenses—from business supplies to international travel. Keep a separate file for assets that you have to depreciate such as large equipment purchases.

Take extra precautions with travel and entertainment expenses. The IRS requires more detailed records for business lunches or trips to attend seminars or meet clients. For each expense, make sure you document the date, the amount you spend, the place, the business purpose, and the business relationship.

For more information on how the IRS is likely to view you, get Publication 937 (800-829-3676). This guide contains 20 factors that will help you determine whether or not you could be considered an employee. In general, to strengthen your case as an independent contractor, you should:

• **Try to comply with as many of the IRS's 20 factors as possible.** For instance, the IRS says that an employee may be trained to perform services, while independent contractors receive no training from clients. In other words, that means that as a self-employed person, you shouldn't take on jobs that you're not qualified to do already. If an assignment requires skills you don't have, you need to secure your own training from a different source such as a community college or an association.

• **Use a business name that's different from your own name.** This helps draw a distinction between you as an individual and your company. For instance, Millie Szerman could have named her public relations business Szerman Inc. or Millie Szerman Services. Instead, she called her company New Directions—a name totally unrelated to her own. This helps her prove that it's her company that is responsible for the work she does.

• **Establish clear contracts with each client.** Spell out in a contract that your company sets its own work hours and that it can terminate services at any time. In other words, you're the one who is in control, not the client.

CHAPTER 6

Marketing Methods for Getting Instant Business

Ah, finally, you're in business. That is, you *have* a business. But there's one small detail you can't exactly overlook: You haven't yet made a *sale*. Okay, so fess up: Does the thought of peddling your product make you feel as if you're about to ask someone out on a first date? If so, you're not alone. Most entrepreneurs, as much as they believe in their products or services, are somewhat hesitant about soliciting business. But as one soloist told us, "If you've gone into business, you've gone into sales." There's just no way around it.

That doesn't mean you have to turn into your plaid-jacket-wearing Uncle Lou—who wouldn't pause at passing out business cards at family funerals. The fact is, Uncle Lou is a man without a plan, firing arrows in every direction. We'll show you how to target your efforts the right way by creating a marketing program with a consistent, effective message aimed at a specific audience: your buyers. Marketing, you'll discover, is much more than knocking on doors and handing out cards. It involves everything you do to sell your product or service, from such tiny details as the color you select for your direct-mail envelope to the full-blown advertising campaign you run on local television. In this chapter, we'll guide you in developing a plan that suits your personality *and* your budget. Most important, we'll help you reach customers by covering such basics as:

- Developing a master plan
- Creating a name that sells
- Launching a direct-marketing campaign
- Advertising on a limited budget
- Generating publicity
- Securing a sale

Develop a Master Plan

If you tapped one of the trends outlined in Chapter 1 or created a product or service that fills an unmet need in society, then you *already* have customers. You simply have to find them—and let them know how to locate you. Of course, tracking down customers can become a complicated, expensive undertaking. And as a small entrepreneur, you can't spare time or money driving down dead-end roads, blaring your message to the wrong audience. You need a well-thought-out, targeted plan to act as your road map.

Unlike a business plan, which may require supporting documents like management bios and research studies, a marketing plan should be simple. Like a map, the more complicated it is, the more difficult it becomes to follow. Later, as you begin to grow and enter new markets, you may want to draw up a more sophisticated blueprint that includes an analysis of the competition. But start with the basics, which we outline below. And keep in mind that the market is always changing— which means you should be ready to modify your plan at any time. Your greatest advantage over large companies, in fact, is your ability to respond pronto to the slightest shift in the economy.

Here's what your marketing program must do:

• **Stress your selling points.** Most important, you must draw as much attention as possible to your business's strengths. What is it that makes your company unique or special? What do you deliver that none of your competitors can match? Home entrepreneur Carmela Cantisani, for instance, created a gourmet French salad dressing that has two key selling points: It's a real olive oil–based French dressing—completely unique from the creamy American variety—and it's low in fat. Cantisani's aim should be to emphasize these special features in every way possible.

• **Focus on your customers.** First off, learn as much as you can about your customers so you can market your product or service to them effectively. What magazines and newspapers do they read? What television programs do they watch? What are their concerns? What do they enjoy doing? (For a refresher on getting to know your customer, go back to Chapter 1.) Next, tell them exactly how your business will benefit them. Will you save them time, money, stress, effort? Your customers want to know what's in it for them.

• **Find the best ways to reach buyers.** Okay, so you know who your customers are and what you want to tell them, but how should you deliver your message? Should you post notices on bulletin boards, create a Web site, or start a direct-mail campaign? Chances are you can come up with dozens of ways to reach your prospects. As you begin to sort through the options we'll tell you about in this chapter, keep in mind that you should select marketing methods that suit your personality. If you're afraid of public speaking, then giving seminars may not be effective for you. But if you have a flair for writing, you could send letters to potential customers or write press releases and magazine articles.

NAMING YOUR BUSINESS

Lesson One: Don't name your business after yourself. Besides the fact that it could be an audit trigger (see Chapter 5), calling your business by your own name doesn't help promote your product or service. Lesley Alderman Inc. or Karen Cheney Enterprises, for instance, could be any kind of business—from apple picking to zoology consulting!

Lesson Two: Your business name should say what you do. Teambuilding consultant Larry Dressler and his partner, for example, call their business Creative Team Solutions. Right away you have an idea what he does. PR pro Millie Szerman helps her clients rev up their business with her company, New Directions. Les Kalmus and Barbara Blair dubbed their temporary services firm specializing in technology CyberStaff America. "Listen to what your customers are asking for and let your name reflect their wants," says Ilise Benun, who runs a home-based newsletter aptly named *The Art of Self Promotion*.

• **Set a budget.** Determine how much you'll spend each quarter or year on your marketing efforts. For instance, you may decide to allocate 20% to 25% of sales to marketing. There's no rule of thumb about how much you should spend. If your primary customer is your former employer, you may not have to spend much money at all. But if you're trying to capture a wider audience, you'll need a larger budget. Just remember that the money you spend marketing your business is an investment, which will pay off in spades if you do it the right way.

• **Track your results.** To figure out what methods work best for you, you need a method for tracking your results. The simplest follow-up is to ask your customers how they heard about you. You can also advertise a special promotion in just one outlet. If sales go up, you know that method worked well. Coupons and 800 numbers are another good way to keep tabs on the effectiveness of a certain ad. If you list a special 800 number in a direct-mail ad and you get a lot of calls, you know that your campaign was a hit.

FOR MORE INFORMATION

• A must-read for home entrepreneurs is *Guerilla Marketing: Secrets for Making Big Profits from Your Small Business* by Jay Conrad Levinson ($12.95; Houghton Mifflin Company).

• Check *Guerilla Marketing*'s Web site (http://www.gmarketing.com), where you can subscribe to a free weekly E-mail newsletter.

• A great tool for market research, *American Demographics* magazine offers a bonanza of free help (http://www.marketingtools.com).

REALITY CHECK—DETERMINING COST

You're no dummy. You want to employ marketing methods that cost the least to reach the most people. For instance, taking out a classified ad in the newspaper may be cheaper than sending out letters to 1,000 potential customers. But if only a handful of people read your ad, it could end up costing you more than the direct-mail campaign.

Here's how you figure cost: Divide the price of your ad, brochure, television commercial, or other marketing effort by the number of people you think will see it. For instance, let's say an advertisement costs you $250 in a local newspaper. If you think that at least 100 potential customers will see the ad, you've spent $2.50 per customer ($250/100 = $2.50).

Direct Marketing:
Going Straight to the Customer

Telemarketing, direct mail, door-to-door selling, and incentives all fall under the rubric "direct marketing." Why? Simple: They're all baits used to hook a potential customer right then and there. We've put direct marketing up front in this chapter because in general, it's a less expensive method to promote sales than advertising in mainstream periodicals or on television and radio. What's more, if you put together a sizzling prospect list, as we explain below, direct marketing is immensely effective. Consider its advantages: You can target your efforts with a surgeon's precision, personalize your messages like crazy, test your techniques for little cost, and track your results with ease.

BUILD A CUSTOMER LIST

Before you can contact your customers, you have to know their addresses, telephone numbers, and other pertinent information about how to reach them. In other words, you need to create a database. Don't worry, you don't have to be a techno-whiz to make one. A database is really just a well-organized address book that you create on your computer using a special software program. Keeping your list up to date is an ongoing process. As your business grows, you should add new categories such as "Past Customers," "Current Customers," and "Hot Prospects." Every time someone shows interest in your business—at a meeting, a seminar, or a trade show, for instance—add that person's name as a prospect. Remember that you'll need to purge your list regularly too, dumping any cold prospects who have failed to show interest once they've been contacted a number of times.

MARKETING ON THE NET

No doubt you've thought about launching your company in cyberspace. After all, the Web is crawling with potential customers. More than 20 million people in North America alone have access to the Internet—and the number is going up every day. What's more, people who surf the Net have high incomes—a whopping 25% of them earn more than $80,000 a year, according to a survey by Nielsen Media Research. And on-line sales are booming.

But beware. You could end up spending more money creating and maintaining a Web site than you'll bring in selling your products. One survey found that fully 23% of businesses on the Web had no sales in the previous month. In fact, to do well on-line, you need to sell certain types of products and services, such as:

Specialty items. If you market hard-to-get products that you can't find in stores, you'll probably do well on-line. For instance, CyberShop (http://www.cybershop.com) peddles high-end items like expensive perfumes and fine china that most stores don't carry. What's more, it doesn't charge for shipping and handling—another incentive for customers to buy.

Internet products and services. Where do customers turn if they are interested in learning about the Internet or establishing a presence on-line? To the Net itself, of course. That means that if you *sell* software, hardware, books, or services that help businesses and individuals set up and maintain sites on-line, you should definitely have your own Web site.

A less expensive—and often more effective—way to promote your business on-line is to spend time schmoozing. Participate in electronic discussion groups and visit specialized salons where you can show off how much you know. When you respond to questions posted on electronic bulletin boards, include your name, business information, and address. If you offer people helpful advice, they're likely to seek out your services in the future.

There are numerous sources for building a list. If you're marketing to your local area, get names from the phone book, Yellow Pages, or chamber of commerce. If your market extends beyond your community, several companies offer CD-ROMs that provide residential and business listings, which can be sorted according to street address, phone number, ZIP code, name, or type of business. Your local library may also have a copy of *Ward's Business Directory of U.S. Private and Public Companies*, which covers more than 130,000 companies representing all industries, and *Directories in Print*, which lists nearly every directory that exists. Don't neglect to troll for potential customers on the World Wide Web, too, by using such business directories as Big Yellow (http://www.bigyellow.com) and Big Book (http://www.bigbook.com).

When Rajan Chaudhry launched *Chain Update*, a newsletter for restaurant chain executives and food service manufacturers, he got names of executives from Securities and Exchange Commission filings. "The filings list all the company officers and directors," says Chaudhry, "so you get their names, addresses, and phone numbers right there." What's more, he points out, SEC filings are updated every year. "Having a high-quality, clean list is very important, because you don't want to waste time and postage on bad addresses," he explains. Another good source of names, says Chaudhry, is a conference directory. "If you attend a conference of chain executives, you get a free booklet with the names and addresses of all the attendees," he says. Once you have the beginnings of a list, you may be able to swap your names with other businesses that serve a market that's related to yours. For instance, caterers and florists sometimes work together on parties and are needed by the same customers.

RENT A LIST

If most of your potential customers belong to a certain professional association, consider renting the organization's mailing list. If you sell camping equipment, for instance, rent lists from outdoor magazines. If your customers are restaurant owners, call the National Restaurant Association. As we explain in Chapter 1, be sure to test the list first by buying only a small number of names.

DIRECT MAIL

Once you have names of prospects, you must determine the best ways to reach them—and direct mail is a favorite approach. No doubt you receive promotional letters every week, if not every day, so you know as well as anyone where most of these pitches end up—in the trash, unopened. In fact, getting a potential customer to take the time to read the contents of your mailing is a huge feat. But if you produce a direct-mail package that clearly and creatively describes the benefits you offer, and target your mailing correctly, you can get fantastic results. We've put together tips from the pros to help you create a winning direct-mail package, beginning with the the most important feature:

The envelope, please. All the careful thought you put into writing an effective sales letter won't matter one lick if the recipient doesn't open the envelope. The envelope that's least likely to wind up in the trash is the most personal-looking one, says Aimee Stern, editor of the newsletter *Marketing Report*. So use a stamp (third class is fine), not a postage meter. "And don't use labels," says Stern. Your best bet is to handwrite the envelope, or if you're mailing hundreds of letters, use a computer font that looks like handwriting. Consider using a colored envelope—particularly yellow or orange, since they stand out the most—or an oversized envelope. "People always open things that look like invitations," adds Stern.

If you opt not to use a personal-looking envelope, use a business one with the word *free* printed on it. People are motivated by emotion, not intellect, says Herschell Gordon Lewis, president of Communicomp, an agency specializing in direct marketing, and author of *Open Me Now*, a primer on direct-mail envelopes. The five biggest motivators, he says, are fear, exclusivity, guilt, the need for approval, and greed. "But the greatest motivator of all," he says, "is greed." There's nothing like stamping FREE OFFER on your envelope to get people to open it. Needless to say, you have to have some kind of giveaway to do so.

The letter. Write those same motivators into your letter. A little guilt, for instance, might sell an insurance policy. After all, "Isn't your family's future worth $1 a day, one day a week?" Or flatter your potential customers by making them feel as if they're part of an exclusive group: "You're one of only 2,052 people with an IQ high enough to read this." (You get the idea!) Such tactics may sound corny, but they work.

Above all, stress the unique benefits of your product or service. We're not saying you should list "100 reasons to buy now." It's far better to isolate a few crucial selling points and drill them into your prospect's head. "We tell our clients to make a logical claim of superiority—if one exists," says Lewis. In other words, don't get carried away calling your cleaning company the only one in town that does carpets and windows unless you're sure that your claim is true. There's no rule as to whether a long letter works better than a short letter or vice versa, but you should stress the benefits you will deliver to the buyer right off the bat. "Fire your biggest gun first," says Lewis. "Don't write a six-page letter and get to the point on page four."

Finally, take care to write your letter in a style your audience will understand. Don't show off your vocabulary, and don't be too technical, even if you're pitching a computer programming service. If your customers were computer savvy, they wouldn't need your service in the first place. Although a spell checker is helpful, make sure you proofread your letter yourself or have several people take a look at it. Spell checkers don't pick up on when you should use "too" rather than "to" or "advise" in place of "advice." Besides proper grammar and vocabulary, take care to find the right tone. If you've never met your prospective customers, be fairly formal. Always address the reader using his or her last name, not first name. It's disrespectful to appear overly chummy. If you don't know to whom you're writing, don't use "Dear Sir." Instead, choose a gender-neutral term like "Dear Human Resources Director."

The response card. Believe it or not, businesses send out sales letters all the time without including the most crucial information: How to obtain the products or services they're pitching. Forcing your prospects to look up your number in the phone book or rummage around for a stamp to write to you is a huge mistake. The more obstacles you throw up, the less likely you'll get a sale. At the very least, include your address and phone number prominently in your sales letter. Or, even better, provide a toll-free number or a stamped, self-addressed response card in each mailing.

When customers start calling, be ready to give them what they want—ASAP. If your prospects need more information, have the appropriate materials, such as a brochure, on hand to send them. Consider using an express delivery service to get your product to them fast. You may even need to hire a part-time assistant to help you out after a direct-mail campaign. On the other hand, what if your response rate is low? The culprit is most likely a bad list. (Remember to test a portion of the names on a list before launching a major campaign.) Besides trying out another list, there are numerous techniques you can use to lure customers. Some of the direct-marketing methods favored by successful home entrepreneurs we interviewed include:

SAMPLING

This is one of the oldest methods of sales promotion, and it's dazzlingly effective. For instance, have you ever walked down a shopping mall and passed a chocolatier giving out scrumptious, bite-sized tidbits? If so, you understand how sampling can whet customers' appetites—sending them straight to the cash register, purchase in hand.

The technique worked especially well for Cory Johnson, president of the home-based business Container Alternatives. Johnson knew he had hit on something gardeners would love when he created Aunt Pudgy's Mix and Mold, a concrete composite powder mix used for making weathered-looking planters, statues, and outdoor wall ornaments. Writing a letter about his product wouldn't be as effective as sending customers a sample, so Johnson placed an ad in a specialized gardening magazine. The ad piqued the interest of many garden-center shops, and Johnson ended up sending out roughly 250 samples.

Of course, you don't have to be a product-oriented business to use sampling. For instance, financial planners may offer a free initial consultation. Consultants may provide a written analysis of a company's new marketing program—at no charge. A carpet-cleaning service might offer a demonstration by doing just one room of a prospect's house. Such freebies can leave customers crying for more.

TRADE SHOWS

Another good place to display your goods *and* give out samples is at a trade show. Johnson attends a string of gardening shows in January and February. "I've found that when people actually watch me mix my product and see how simple it is, then it really sells itself," he says. Trade shows are invaluable if your business requires a demonstration. Plus, they're teeming with manufacturers, suppliers, retailers, and end users whom you would have a hard time meeting otherwise.

INCENTIVES

Sales, discounts, special offers, and contests all qualify as incentives because they make buyers out of prospects. In fact, an incentive is simply a little nudge that pushes a prospective customer right into your lap. Fitness centers, for instance, gain members by offering one month free to folks who sign up now. Video stores use punch-card systems that allow you to pick out a movie at no charge once you've rented 10 movies. Major airlines offer frequent-flyer programs. Before you launch an incentive program, though, carefully calculate its costs and benefits. If you get carried away, you could actually end up losing money. Above all, keep your offer simple. It needs to be easy to understand and readily attainable. People won't sign on to a movie rental program that requires them to watch 100 videos before they get a single one for free.

TELEMARKETING

No, we don't advocate calling everyone on your database right around dinner hour. But we do think that telemarketing can be an effective tool for you if used correctly. To make it work, you need a very targeted list of prospective customers—what Lewis calls "the tip of the pyramid." You may even decide to call only those individuals who have done business with you in the past—or those who have shown a strong interest in your business. A financial planner, for instance, might call people who attended seminars he offered at the local community center to see if they would like further assistance.

When making a call, identify yourself, your business, and, most important, the benefit you're offering. In other words, let the person on the other end of the line know right away what he or she will gain by talking to you. And don't mask the call as a survey. It's best to be straightforward. To engage the listener, you should ask questions about his or her needs and listen to the answers you receive. Scripted calls typically don't work well. No matter what, you'll experience a lot of rejection. But keep in mind that telemarketing takes less time than a letter and it's more difficult for customers to say no to you directly.

ASK FOR REFERRALS

Talk to established home entrepreneurs and they'll tell you that most of their business comes by word of mouth. "Ah, to be at a point where business simply comes to me," you're thinking. You may be surprised to learn that most successful soloists actually *ask* for referrals. True, some satisfied customers will naturally turn into a walking, talking sales force, but more often, you'll have to let them know that you appreciate and thrive on referrals. Of course, don't neglect to take good care of customers who boost your business. Consider giving them an incentive, such as a gift certificate or discount. And make it easy for them to refer more business to you by providing them with extra copies of your brochures and business cards.

FOR MORE INFORMATION

• *Your Company* magazine, published six times a year by Time Inc. and American Express Publishing Corp., is jam-packed with creative marketing ideas (free to corporate card holders, $4 an issue for noncard holders; 800-528-2122).
• Home business gurus Paul and Sarah Edwards, along with Laura Clampitt Douglas, offer an excellent guide in *Getting Business to Come to You* ($11.95; Jeremy P. Tarcher/Putnam).
• Pricey but worth it, *The Marketing Report* is a favorite newsletter among pros. It claims 20,000 marketing directors as readers ($264 for 22 issues, 800-220-5000).
• Herschell Gordon Lewis has written more than a dozen books on marketing. Two good ones: *Open Me Now* ($40; Bonus

Books), a primer on direct-mail envelopes, and *Sales Letters that Sizzle* ($29.95; National Textbook Company).

Creating Low-Cost, Effective Ads

You may think that advertising is off limits for you. After all, companies like Coca-Cola, Calvin Klein, and AT&T spend millions of dollars every year on television commercials, radio spots, and splashy outdoor bulletin boards. But you don't have to bust your budget to promote your business with advertising. There are many low-cost methods that will work even better for you than a $100,000, one-second TV spot during the Super Bowl. Fact is, most self-employed individuals either market to a very specialized audience or they target their local area. That means they don't need to throw money away on a massive campaign. So unless you're marketing to the general public, you'll find that your efforts are best spent on one or all of the following ad venues:

SIGNS

If zoning laws in your area permit, one of the simplest things you can do is to put up a sign in front of your house. This works well if you're marketing to your local community. And of course, it also helps if you live in an area that gets a fair amount of traffic. If your house is on a quiet cul-de-sac, then sticking a sign in your yard won't bring you a bonanza of business. But as long as potential customers frequent your area, why not? Just make sure you have the sign made professionally, or, if you do it yourself, use stencils. And be sure to include a telephone number.

KEEP IT LEGAL

Whether you're creating fliers to hand out, placing a full-page ad in a consumer magazine, or merely posting notices on bulletin boards, be aware that you're legally responsible for your ads and the claims you make in them. A false ad, according to the Federal Trade Commission, is one that contains an outright lie, fails to disclose a significant fact, or creates an overall false impression.

You've probably seen millions of ads, for instance, promoting face cream. But did you ever notice how the ads claim that using the product with help to "diminish the appearance" of wrinkles, rather than get rid of them altogether? It's a subtle but important distinction. You must be equally careful in your choice of words. While you don't want to use a watered-down expression like "We'll try our best to help you," you shouldn't say, "We're ready to help you 24 hours a day" unless it's true.

Even if your ad doesn't contain a false statement, it could create an overall false impression. To reduce the chance of running afoul of the law, ask your friends to take an objective look at your ads. And no matter what, if you claim that your service or product will achieve a certain result, make sure you have proof to back up your statement.

For More Information:

Call the FTC's Public Reference Branch and order two sets of policy papers: *Advertising Policy on Ad Substantiation* and *Advertising Policy on Deception* (free; 202-326-2222).

THE YELLOW PAGES

If you offer a brand-new type of product or service—say, an unusual invention or a novel use for technology—the Yellow Pages won't be of much use to you. That's because people typically turn to their phone books to look up familiar types of businesses. But if your business fits in a category that's already being used in the Yellow Pages, then getting a listing could boost your sales. Keep in mind that there's no one single directory. Several companies may produce Yellow Pages in your area, and you may find that there are different editions—for the metropolitan area and the suburbs, for instance. So focus on the location of your target market when you select your outlet.

Of course, to get a listing, you have to have a business phone line. Next, set up an appointment with a sales rep to discuss your alternatives. For instance, you may want to list your business under several headings for cross-referencing purposes. The toughest decision is choosing the size. Your impulse may be to take out a big display ad, but be careful not to overspend. Large ads may inspire more calls but not necessarily more business. Most important, you want an ad that's big enough to state your benefits without looking crowded. Include a phone number, a fax number, and even an E-mail address if you think customers are likely to reach you via computer.

TRADE DIRECTORIES

If you offer a more specialized business-to-business service, you may be better off going with a trade or specialty directory. Your library should contain references like *Directories in Print*, which we mentioned earlier in this chapter. You'll also find that every trade and professional organization has a membership directory. If you join the Institute of Management Consultants, for instance, you can be listed in its directory, which many businesses use to find help for special projects.

CLASSIFIED ADS

You can find classified ads in newspapers, trade journals, many consumer magazines, and even newsletters. What do your customers tend to read? Are they gourmet cooks likely to pick up a copy of *Chef* magazine or doctors who get their news from publications like *Medical Economics*? With a home-based medical billing business, Robert O'Kelly, for instance, wisely places his ads in medical directories and publications delivered to doctors' offices.

Budget permitting, you can go for a fancy display ad. But classifieds have advantages too—namely, they tend to attract readers who are already looking for services and products to buy. They're typically priced by the word, line, or column inch, and sometimes you have the choice between a words-only ad and a mini–display ad in which you could even feature your own photograph. As with writing a sales letter, you need to use active verbs and play on emotions like exclusivity or greed that help you sell your goods. Remember: Focus on your customers and the benefits you offer them that your competitors don't.

LOCAL TELEVISION AND RADIO

The best way to promote your business on radio and TV is to have the news media put you there for free. We'll tell you how to do that in the next section. But don't discard the notion of using paid advertising to take advantage of the airwaves too, particularly if you want to reach a wide audience. Radio is particularly good at helping you establish an intimate relationship with your prospective customers. Plus, you can use music and other sound effects to make your message more memorable. Local cleaning services, day-care providers, and speaking coaches, for instance, can use radio to great success. Choose your station just as you would choose a magazine in which to place a print ad. That is, go with the one that your prospects listen to regularly—whether it's reggae, rock, or talk news.

What about TV? Thanks to community-access channels, small businesses are raising their profile on this medium, too. Advertising is prohibited on these channels, which are set aside to broadcast local events such as city council meetings and school activities. But if you sponsor local programming, you can usually display your business name and logo at the beginning and end of a program. Contact your local cable provider to check out rates for producing your own show, too. This is especially effective for catering, flower arranging, or other highly visual businesses. Cable operators with more than 35 channels are required to set aside time for independent programming (otherwise known as "leased access"). But beware: The cable company doesn't like to give up prime-time hours, so it may only offer slots in the wee hours when your customers are still sound asleep.

FOR MORE INFORMATION

• The Federal Communications Commission's Cable Services Bureau in Washington, D.C., provides information on commercial leased-access rules. Check out its Web site (http://www.fcc.gov).

Generating Free Publicity

When an article in *The Wall Street Journal* quotes home entrepreneur Rajan Chaudhry, he knows he's going to spend a day on the phone. "I get at least a dozen calls," says Chaudhry, editor and publisher of the weekly newsletter *Chain Update* (mentioned earlier in this chapter). Of course, who's complaining? When his name appears in print, Chaudhry gains new subscribers and, just as important, prestige. "Being quoted in the *Journal* builds your credibility and your reputation," he says. And that's what publicity is all about. It helps establish you and your business in the marketplace, making your name the one people look for when they need the goods or services you offer.

Being quoted in the newspaper is just one way of planting yourself and your business in the minds of your customers. You can also sponsor community events, give free seminars, and participate in your chamber of commerce. All such activities create a positive image of your business—in other words, they generate good PR. In this section, we'll show you how to halve your marketing expenses with free publicity and fantastic PR.

NETWORK

If you run a service-oriented company, you're likely to gain more business from people you've met at club meetings, open house parties, or conferences than you will by launching an expensive ad campaign. People like to do business with someone they know and trust, and if you're active in a community group or trade organization, you fit that profile. Of course, we don't advocate joining every social and business group in town. For starters, you don't have time for that. But more important, participating in the local knitting circle isn't going to help your computer services business. Instead, you should carefully select organizations where you're most likely to meet potential customers. Tom Wotherspoon, a freelance broadcast advertising producer, for instance, meets clients regularly by attending functions sponsored by the Advertising Federation and participating in the Florida Advertising Golfers Association.

CATCH THE MEDIA'S ATTENTION

If talking up your business is good, having an objective party promote it is even better. But what magic must you work to grab the media's attention? Hardly any at all. You don't need to hire an expensive PR rep or even print up a fancy press kit. Getting a TV spot or having your name mentioned in print takes little more than common sense, courtesy, and a good nose for a story. To bring you behind the curtain, we asked journalists around the country about whom they write about and why. And, of course, as writers for **MONEY** magazine, we have plenty of tips to share with you, too.

Target your efforts. First off, figure out which publications would be most interested in hearing from you. If your market doesn't extend beyond your town or region, focus on local newspapers, city magazines, and perhaps a statewide magazine. Of course, it never hurts to have the national media take notice of you too. So browse the newsstand and find publications in your field. If you're a travel agent, put *Condé Nast Traveler* and *Travel & Leisure* on your mailing list. Your clients will be impressed when a national magazine quotes you, and you may gain more business. If you're a financial planner, put **MONEY** magazine on your list. As writers for **MONEY** magazine, we're always looking for new sources—such as financial planners, CPAs, and other experts whom we can call in a pinch.

Next, determine *whom* to call or write. Rather than ring the city desk of a newspaper and ask for any reporter who's available, request a specific person. Make sure you've read that reporter's work and are familiar with his or her beat and favorite topics. "I get a lot of misguided press releases that have nothing to do with what I cover," says *Newsweek* correspondent Martha Brant. "Sometimes they don't even have my name spelled right."

Pitch a story, not your business. We get hundreds of phone calls, letters, and press releases from PR people, financial planners, and businesses every week, all pitching stories. Which ones do we notice? Truth is, not many. In fact, probably 80% of the releases we receive make a clean shot into the wastebasket. What's the problem? Most likely the story is old news, or the person writing to us wants us to profile his or her business. Lesson One: The national news media doesn't give a lick about your business. Even the local paper will sniff at writing about you unless you have a unique story.

So what does the press like to write about?

• **Trends.** Let's say you're a private investigator—an interesting field to be in but not necessarily worthy of a story. But then let's say you begin to notice a trend in your business—say, that the majority of your new clients are men in their forties spying on their exes. Now you've got a story. But perhaps you can go even farther. What if you called a few other investigators and found that they had a large number of clients just like yours? You'd have one heck of a juicy story. Journalists love trends, and not just tantalizing ones with men spying on their exes. A CPA might notice that a number of his clients are having difficulties with the same item in the tax code. Travel agents may observe that more people are flying to England this year, thanks to a spurt of Jane Austen movies. Or a computer sales rep might notice that demand is particularly hot for a certain product.

• **Scams.** Since journalists fancy themselves watchdogs for the nation, they love uncovering frauds of any type. If you're aware of any questionable practices going on in your field, contact the media. Even if you don't want your name in print for confidentiality reasons, you'll establish a strong bond with the reporter.

• **News.** If you're going to make significant changes to your business that will affect the community, you've created news. For instance, you may plan to expand your services and hire new people. Although you can't expect attention from the national media, you should let your local paper know about your plans. On the other hand, if you invent a new product that's likely to have a national impact, you should contact everyone from the *New York Times* on down.

• **Service.** Cruise by a local newsstand and you'll notice that many publications are devoted to service journalism—that is, they don't simply give readers the news, they tell them what to do with it. For instance, when the stock market gets the jitters, MONEY magazine tells readers how to protect their portfolios by buying certain types of securities. Health, travel, general business, and trade magazines also aim to give readers information they can apply to their lives. Do you have any tips that readers would want to hear? "If someone has an idea that I think would be helpful to my readers, I'll figure out a way to get it in the magazine," says Susie Stephenson, a senior editor with *Restaurants & Institutions*, one of the nation's largest trade magazines. For instance, let's say you run a catering business out of your home and you discover a great new way to keep food warm during deliveries. This is practical information that the right publication would like to print.

One more thing: Be sensitive about deadlines. Most newspapers come out in the morning. That means deadlines begin in the late afternoon. Never call during this time; instead, stick to mornings. And no matter what, ask the reporter if he or she is busy, and if so, find out when you can call back.

Offer your expertise. If you can't think of a trend, scam, or other story to pitch, you can always offer your expertise for future articles. In this case, it's best to write a letter, telling the reporter that you're available for help on certain topics. If you're a CPA, for instance, let the reporter know you'll crunch numbers at any time for special charts and graphs. If you're a psychologist, write to a reporter who covers health and medicine and suggest yourself as a source for stories on depression, eating disorders, or whatever your specialty is.

Say something interesting. Be quotable. Most business people are so caught up in their particular specialty that they have a hard time talking to an average Joe. They throw in technical terms, become bureaucratic, or sound stiff and formal. If you know how to use colorful, everyday language and speak in complete sentences, reporters will have your telephone number memorized in no time.

Be reliable. If you get a message from a reporter, call back ASAP. Chances are the reporter is on a tight deadline, so if you wait an hour or two, you'll be out of luck. Reporters simply spin their Rolodexes until they get someone on the line who can answer their questions. Most important, give accurate information. If a reporter asks you a question and you're not sure about the answer, don't try to bluff your way through it. Either the reporter will see through to your ignorance, or, worse, your name will go into print attached to an erroneous statement. You'll look stupid, and the reporter will never call you again. Instead, tell the reporter you'll try to find what he or she is looking for and will call back right away.

DRAW ON YOUR EXPERTISE

Don't rely on reporters alone to establish you as an expert in a field. Write your own articles and editorials or produce your own newsletter! To write for magazines, send a query letter suggesting several story ideas, and let the editor know what special insights you would bring to the piece. The best way to break into a newspaper is by writing an editorial. Most papers like editorials about current news topics. For instance, if your business is in home health care, you might write about the changing landscape of medical care.

If you don't have a flair for writing, consider offering a seminar or giving a speech to one of the organizations to which you belong. You may gain valuable contacts—and even spur new business. Garrett Ludwig, for instance, has a special niche designing dentists' offices. "When I need business, direct mail is a waste of time," says Ludwig. "The people I work for invest many, many thousands of dollars with me, so they need to build up trust." To help gain their confidence and get to know his potential clients better, Ludwig sometimes gives seminars on dental office planning. To further boost his profile in the industry, he publishes articles in dental and medical trade journals.

GIVE SOMETHING BACK

When you sponsor a community event, take part in fund-raising activities for special-interest groups, or support the high school football team, you show that you have higher goals than making money. And you build a positive image of your company. Elizabeth Cyran of Silver Ridge Photography, for instance, does pro bono work for animal groups by snapping shots of people's pets. "Everybody wants to know that you're a nice person," says Cyran. "And if you do volunteer work, people view you as being community-oriented."

FOR MORE INFORMATION

• Ilise Benun shares her tips once a quarter in her newsletter *The Art of Self Promotion* ($30; P.O. Box 23, Hoboken NJ 07030).

• Statewide media guides with names and numbers of press members are available in many states. Check with your local library and bookstore.

Tips for Clinching a Sale

Now it's time to close a big deal—but do you have to turn into an aggressive sales pro to do so? Relax. Selling is not synonymous with bulldozing. In fact, building a relationship with a client is much like forming a friendship. You have to get to know the client, listen to his or her needs, and gradually establish trust. This process may take more time with some of your customers than others. Remember that clients are people—and no two people are alike. Of course, you will meet with rejection. Getting jilted is part of the job. But if you follow these steps, you're far more likely to clinch the sale.

GET TO KNOW YOUR CLIENTS—BEFORE YOU EVEN MEET THEM

What's the best way to catch your prospects' attention? Let them know how smart and insightful you are! This calls for some homework. First, hit the library, the Internet, the telephone—whatever it takes to learn all you can about a specific prospect. If you want to sell your services to a certain business, find out what that company's strengths and shortcomings are. Are competitors invading its market niche? What is the overall industry like in which the company operates? "When I have appointments with companies, I like to visit their Web site and have some information when I go in," says home-based manufacturer's representative Suzy Murray.

When you feel as if you have a good grasp on your prospect's situation, write a letter in which you pinpoint the problems the company faces. Then suggest a meeting to discuss the issues in further depth. If you don't get a response within two weeks, don't panic. You'll probably need to follow up with a phone call or two. Remember that it may take several contacts before you're actually able to set up a meeting.

LET YOUR PROSPECTS TELL YOU HOW TO MAKE THE SALE

When the meeting you've longed for finally arrives, don't get the jitters and start chattering like an auctioneer. You've already demonstrated your knowledge. Now let the prospect do the talking. By listening to the CEO explain how the company works, you'll learn what his or her concerns really are. In other words, you'll find out exactly how to tailor your services to meet your prospect's needs.

DELIVER A PERSONAL PITCH

Now that you know what's eating at your prospect, you're ready to offer your services. But don't pull out the same song-and-dance act you did for your last customer. Employee trainer David Spivey says that most of his colleagues use packaged training programs. "It's very costly in terms of time to develop your own materials," he explains. But it's important to personalize the materials for different customers, he says. After all, your prospect will sense it if you give him or her a routine spiel. Even if your new prospect has problems very similar to a former client's, you need to customize your sales pitch. So tap the concerns the CEO raised—you can even use his or her very same words. If you address the exact issues the prospect brought up and provide compelling solutions, congratulations—you've clinched a sale.

FOR MORE INFORMATION

• *Selling for Dummies* by Tom Hopkins offers practical and effective techniques for even the most tongue-tied salesperson ($16.99; IDG Books Worldwide).

CHAPTER 7

Succeeding on
Your Own

Going solo might be one of the most liberating experiences of your entire career—maybe even your life. But then too, it may also be one of the most terrifying. True, you're free from the manacles of a regular job, those bad bosses, rigid schedules, and tiresome meetings. But you're also free from many of the *comforting* structures of corporate life, like supportive colleagues, firm deadlines, and a steady paycheck.

How do you make the transition from tethered employee to captain of your own ship? Well, success, in part, starts in your mind. Call it an entrepreneurial bent, a creative edge, or a stubborn resolve; whatever the phrase, it comes down to a belief that you can *and want* to make it on your own. Psychologists who have studied entrepreneurs and what makes them tick refer to this solo sensibility as having an "internalized locus of control." In plain English, this means you believe you can master the events of the world, rather than feeling that events master you. "The more you can adopt the mind-set that you have the ability to make things happen," says psychologist Dr. Robert Lefton of Psychological Associates, "the more tenacious and ambitious—and therefore the more successful—you will be."

But you need more than highfalutin psychological concepts to be successful. You need concrete methods and strategies. To help you learn how to manage and run your new business, and thereby develop your sense of mastery and power, we turned to scores of home-based entrepreneurs as well as self-employment experts. Based on their suggestions and ideas (and our own home office expertise) we offer you advice in three broad areas:

- Your work life
- Your clients
- Your home life

Managing Your Work

Hands down, the biggest challenge new entrepreneurs face is coping with the insecurity of flying solo. How are you going to handle all those moments of self-doubt? What do you do when the economic horizon looks bleak? How do you deal with the isolation of self-employment? Answer: You micromanage your work life. That doesn't mean being a control freak. It simply means anticipating problems before they arise.

SET SHORT- AND LONG-TERM GOALS

Self-discipline is essential when you're starting out. The best way to stay focused and use your time well? Set goals. Start with your long-term objectives and then break them down into short-term tasks. Start by writing a one-to-three-sentence mission statement for your company. It can be as broadly ambitious as "My goal is to offer the best personalized service to my clients and make $100,000 a year." Or it can be as targeted as

"My obejctive is to write 10 feature stories this year for a national magazine." The point is this: Get your objective down on paper. Then create goals that will get you there. Katie LaChance, president of Legal Services Institute, says it helps her to work backwards. "I look at what I want to accomplish for the year and then I decide what to do each day to achieve those goals." For instance, LeChance might decide over a period of three months that she needs to talk to 20 people to get seven clients. "Then I break it down into daily tasks," she says. "Once you write down what you want to achieve it just starts happening."

CREATE A REALISTIC SCHEDULE

After you've set your goals, create a schedule to put them into action. Your best strategy is to stick to your old routine—at least for starters. If you're used to rising at 6 A.M., running for a half hour, and then sitting down to work at 8 A.M., then do that. Establish a structure that keeps you focused. Anyone who has worked at home for a day, a month, or even years can tell you about the numerous temptations to lure you away from the job at hand. There's always something you missed in the refrigerator, an Oprah show that needs watching, and, of course, that lawn is looking a little shabby. Forget it. And don't even kid yourself about that "have-laptop-will-travel" syndrome. That's a dream, one that lulls you into thinking you can work just as efficiently at the beach house or the corner coffee shop as you can in your home office. Plenty of pros swear they can work anywhere. But wait until your business is hurrying along before you start hurrying off with your laptop to sip latte.

Once you have a schedule, you can start to micromanage your day. Write up your daily to-do list and start moving toward your goals. Assign each task a specific time frame. It may sound simplistic, but trust us, it works. If you think best in the morning, then reserve writing or planning for the early hours. If you burn out by 4 P.M., save that time for the mindless tasks, like opening mail and returning phone calls. The more you structure your day, the less likely you will be distracted by frivolous activities like cleaning out the linen closet or rearranging the furniture.

TIME MANAGEMENT TOOLS

If self-discipline and organization are not your forté, admit your weaknesses and seek advice from experts. These tools can help you get on track:

Books

First Things First by Stephen R. Covey ($23.00; Simon & Schuster)

Time Management for Dummies by Jeffrey J. Mayer ($16.99; IDG Books)

Time Tactics of Very Successful People by B. Eugene Griessman ($15.00; McGraw-Hill; 800-722-4726)

Software

Sidekick 97 (Starfish; 888-STARFISH) has a calendar, Rolodex, expense report function, and an alarm to remind you of important meetings.

Day-Timer Organizer (Day-Timer Technologies; 800-535-4242). An easy-to-use electronic organizer that manages to-do lists, contacts, and expenses.

Advice givers

National Association of Professional Organizers (NAPO) 512-206-0151. Provides referrals to professional organizers around the country.

Try gimmicks like daily planners, software programs, or Post-its on your computer. Experiment to find tools that suit your style. If you're a computer fanatic, a fancy electronic organizer may be just the ticket. But if you're the visual type, you may prefer a Filofax with color-coded tabs. One last tip: When making lists, be specific and prioritize. Have an "A" list of what *must* be done and a "B" list of what *could* be done.

Lastly, nip those time-wasting habits in the bud. Azriela Jaffe, author of *Honey, I Want to Start My Own Business*, said her husband finally had to admit that working at home was not for him. A consummate handyman and tinkerer, he would find himself drifting off after lunch to fix the broken toilet or repair the sprinkler system. After six months, he gave in and found an office far from home enticements.

CREATE SUPPORT NETWORKS

People need people. This is especially true when they work at home alone. You need contacts to trade war stories, discuss ideas, and keep your competitive juices flowing. One way to do this is to form your own professional support group. Says consultant Larry Dressler, "When I lived in Los Angeles, I had two informal but regularly scheduled 'tea' meetings with other entrepreneurs. One of the meetings involved three other self-employed consultants, the other consisted of home-based businesspeople. We would discuss everything from strategies for handling collections problems to how home business was affecting personal relationships. Call it a support group or dialogue. They were extremely useful."

If you don't have a peer group, join an existing one. The American Association of Home Based Businesses (AAHBB) (800-447-9710) has numerous chapters around the country. If there isn't one in your area, the AAHBB can give you advice on how to start one. Likewise, write to the National Business Incubation Association (NBIA, 20 East Circle Drive, Suite 190, Athens, OH 45701) to find a networking group of small business owners in your area. You can also reach them on the Web: www.nbia.org.

Cyberspace is another great place for get-togethers. Don't discount the virtual network. If you are housebound or if you just want to increase your professional contacts, get on the Internet chat circuit. All the major on-line services have message boards where you can post questions. And you never have to worry about who picks up the tab for the coffee. For general home-business concerns, CompuServe's Working From Home Forum (GO WORK) is excellent. It's one of the most popular sources for home workers who are just starting out. Beverly Rose, who runs a secretarial support business, says she learned everything she needed to know about starting her business by posting queries on the Working From Home bulletin boards. For specific information on your business, check out UseNetNews on the Internet. It's an excellent resource. Jeff Yoak, an internet developer, spends seven to ten hours a week at UseNetNews reading queries from colleagues about new developments on Web design. Says Yoak, "There's a real spirit of sharing."

But networking, whether in the coffee house or over the Internet, is not the only way to stay in touch with colleagues. You can also teach, do public speaking, write articles, or volunteer with local business associations. The point is to "have some kind of affiliation," advises stay-at-home children's book author Eric Arnold. Arnold, who taught school for 14 years, takes two hours off during the day to teach at the local public school. "You need to get out of the house and be with people who share your interest and values," he says. Teaching also gives Arnold a chance to be with "his public": the children who will someday read his books. To get feedback, he often reads them sections from his writing. The effect: an instant focus group.

Ultimately, you need to find a way to feel connected to the world beyond your own office door. Without social contact the catty office politics you happily left behind may start to seem mighty appealing. Rule One: Get out of the house. Not for long, but just to clear your head. Run an errand, do lunch, chat with the guy at the dry cleaner's. (Warning: This is not an excuse to play hooky.) Consultant Larry Dressler has devised a unique, if unusual, ritual. He has placed his mailbox 15 minutes away from his Olympia, Washington, home. This ensures that he will have to make a "daily round-trip pilgrimage" of 30 minutes each day. Along the way he gets to see new faces. Meanwhile, Cambridge-based consultant Paul O'Malley walks to a local coffee shop for breakfast. There he's assured quality social time chatting with regulars about the weather, the Red Sox, or local elections. And the ten-minute walk is a nice way to stretch his legs.

MARKET CONSTANTLY

Every entrepreneur gets the jitters—those days when the phone just won't ring, your top client tells you he's bankrupt, or you realize the response to your $5,000 direct-mail piece was nil. You'll wring your hands, recheck your bank balance, and start dreaming up an exit strategy. Unless, of course, you've been smart and have been marketing your business all along. You can reduce the panic and the terrifying instability of self-employment by marketing constantly. You should spend at least 25% of your time hunting for new business—*even* when business is going well. Devote a portion of each day to courting new clients and servicing the old (for marketing tips see Chapter 6).

Another technique to reduce the tension: diversify. Some soloists find it helpful to have a part-time job outside their home office that provides a steady paycheck and built-in structure. Kim Palmer, a part owner in a custom publishing business, works part time as an editor for the *Minneapolis Star Tribune*. Rob Anthony, a personal finance writer, added a second profession. He became a tax preparer to increase his income and add a new challenge. During the tax season he works on his clients' returns. The rest of the year he writes. One of the advantages of self-employment is that you can create a patchwork of jobs that fits your work style and interests.

ASK FOR HELP

You went into business so *you* could call all the shots. But some days you realize you don't know what all those shots are. Instead of being stubborn, call for help. "Entrepreneurs develop an 'I can do it myself' attitude," notes Beverly Williams, president of the American Association of Home Based Businesses. "This becomes a problem if they waste time on tasks that could be done more efficiently by others." For instance, you've read this entire book, and say, "No sweat, I can do this by myself." And you probably can. But can you do everything *well*? It might be worth the extra $1,000 to get a professional marketing pro to write ad copy if writing is simply not your strong suit. Likewise, before you decide to purchase a new PC system, consider running your idea by another home-business PC wizard, or hiring a consultant for an hour to give you ace advice. The point: Spend your time doing what you do best and don't be afraid to ask the pros for help.

Now don't get us wrong. We're not telling you to spend your hard-earned profits on high-priced consultants. Often you can find basic advice from your network of professional contacts or by posting a query to an on-line bulletin board, such as the Working From Home Forum or Your Business on America Online. For big-picture business help, the box in Chapter 3 on page 71 can refer you to free small business consultants. But, when it comes to your business, you should be ready to shell out extra bucks for expert advice. Often it can make your business more profitable and efficient. Remember the adage: Sometimes you have to spend money to make money.

FOR MORE INFORMATION

• *Working Solo* by Terry Lonier ($14.95, Portico Press; 800-222-7656)

• *Making It On Your Own: Surviving and Thriving the Ups and Downs of Being Your Own Boss* by Paul and Sarah Edwards ($11.95; Jeremy Tarcher/Perigee).

• *National Association for the Self Employed* (NASE). Benefits include a toll-free advice hot line, newsletter, and discounts on over 100 services. Cost to join: $72 a year (800-232-NASE).

• *American Association of Home Based Businesses* (800-447-9710) has local chapters, a newsletter, and conferences.

Managing Your Clients

A few months into self-employment and you might long for the days when your boss handed you a stack of work and you simply did it. No customers to court, no bills to collect, no contracts to negotiate. But look on the bright side: once your business starts to soar, you'll be able to turn away nasty clients or refuse work that doesn't thrill you.

SET A PROFESSIONAL IMAGE

Okay, so you like to work in cutoffs and a T-shirt. Fine. That's one of the bonuses of working from home. However, you still have to present a professional image to the world when the world comes to call. That doesn't mean you have to appear at every meeting in pumps and silk blouses or wing tips and a blue blazer. It does mean you have to look professional.

If you have clients visiting your home office, make the space impressive and comfortable. Katie LaChance covered her office wall with framed articles about her company from prominent magazines. You can hang your diplomas, display your trophies, and flaunt your awards, too. Just think how confident you feel when you visit a doctor who has impressive, gold-framed diplomas covering his walls. You're not likely to see his tie thrown over a chair or his shoes tossed off in a corner. Keep your own office free from that same personal detritus. Tuck away all those artifacts of daily living, like the laundry basket, your dog's bone, and your kid's ragged ragdoll. Otherwise clients may get the idea that your business, and hence *their* projects, take a backseat to family life.

Working from home used to have a stigma. There was the suspicion that you were either out of work or a wacko who couldn't make it in the "real world." But that's not so anymore. People who work from home are now seen as spirited and entrepreneurial. In fact, clients "may perceive they get value added by using the services of someone who works from home," observes small business consultant Gene Fairbrother. Yes, your business should have all the attributes of a Fortune 500 company: classy stationery, smart business cards, and a professional answering service. (By the way, no cute messages on the answering machine.) But it's also good to strike a balance. That means keep it smart, but also keep a personal touch. An intimate professionalism can attract clients—and ultimately keep them coming back for more.

MEET YOUR NEW BOSS: YOUR CLIENT

"Gosh," you think, "I thought you just told me I was my own boss." Well not completely. As Joe Anthony likes to joke, "Now I have a hundred bosses, instead of one." Your clients are the lifeblood of your business and you should take their pulse regularly. There are two reasons for this: First, to establish good customer relations; second, to get information on how you are doing. Think of each customer as a partner. They are going to supply you with a problem or project and you are going to help them solve it. They want you to succeed as much as you do. So when one project is over, give them a quick call or even write a letter. Ask what went well, what did not, and what advice they would give to improve your services or product. Each client gives you a unique opportunity to fine-tune your business procedures.

DRAW UP WRITTEN CONTRACTS

Whether your client is your brother-in-law, your former boss, or your next-door neighbor, spell out the terms of your agreements—in writing. The contract can be a simple letter that states the service you agree to perform, when you will complete it, how long it will take, and how much it will cost. Depending on the nature of the project and how much money it will involve, it can be a formal document that you and the client both sign. Your contract should include specific information on how you will be paid and on what date.

On the other hand, if the client gives *you* a contract, consider attaching an addendum or drawing up a separate agreement of your own. Why? Freelance writers are typically asked to sign a standard contract supplied by the magazine or newspaper. But in addition, the writer might attach a letter that spells out how much time they will spend on the project, when they will be available for follow-up questions, and how many revisions they are prepared to do. While it might seem controlling and mistrustful at first to use a contract, most clients will realize that you are simply being a consummate professional. If they balk, you may want to reconsider your relationship with them. When you're starting out, ask colleagues for samples of their contracts. If you are a professional like an architect or consultant, your trade organization will have samples you can use.

BE ASSERTIVE ABOUT MONEY

It's an onerous task: calling clients to ask them to pay up. But it's a skill most small business owners need to acquire. It's not like you're selling encyclopedias door to door. You have what someone wants. And they agreed to pay you for it. So why not ask? Women especially feel squeamish about talking cash with clients. But remind yourself of this: No matter how much you like (or even dislike) your clients, this is a business transaction and not a personal transaction. You have performed a service, and now you need to be paid. If a client is consistently unable to pay on time, it's time to say sayonara. No matter how much you love what you do, you are in business to make a profit. Tell yourself that again and again each day. If you're still not convinced, take a look at your bank balance.

Balancing Business and Family

One of the reasons you probably chose to work at home was to spend more time with your family, or, if you're single, to weave your personal and professional lives together in a less stressful way. Instead of wasting time kibbitzing at the coffee machine, you can now use your "coffee breaks" to throw in a load of laundry or help your child with her homework. But working at home can cause conflicts with family and friends. To carve out a successful place for your at-home business, you need clear boundaries.

TALK ABOUT THE BUSINESS WITH FAMILY AND FRIENDS

As you will soon learn, if the lesson hasn't come to you already, new business owners sometimes become obsessed with their work. And this can really stress out your relationships—with your spouse, your kids, your friends. To avoid personal conflicts, have an honest talk with all these people—kids included—about your hopes and goals and the pressures you are facing. The more you let your loved ones know what to expect, the less chance for conflict down the line.

YOUR FRIENDS

"Gee, now that you're working at home we can have lunch together," your stay-at-home friends might say. Sure, but when you up and leave after an hour to get back to work, be prepared for raised eyebrows—and not a few sour looks. Says author Azriela Jaffe, "When I end a lunch date with friends they often take it personally or think I'm being too type A." When you're working at home, friends have a tendency to think you've got time on your hands. It's up to you to set them straight. Tell them your new schedule is just as demanding as an office job, even more so. If you're pulling late-nighters, week after week, warn them that you won't be available for movies and long phone chats. But tell them that you're looking forward to seeing them when work clears. And if your new business is putting a crimp in your budget, let your pals know in advance that dinners out may have to be at Au Bon Pain rather than the latest French bistro.

YOUR SPOUSE

It's inevitable. The stress of starting a new business and the financial finaglings that come with it can put a strain on even the strongest marriage. For starters, your beloved may now assume that since you're home you can run errands or vacuum the house before company arrives. Not so, say authors Ellen Parlapiano and Patricia Cobe. For their book, *Mompreneurs*, they interviewed over a hundred work-at-home moms. The number one complaint: "My husband wants me to pick up his dry cleaning." Be very clear from the outset what you can and cannot take on. Discuss all the potential land mines, like child care, house chores, errands, and even doing the laundry. "One of the biggest mistakes," says Jaffe, "is that couples underestimate the impact the business will have on their relationships." This is especially true when it comes to finances. So be prepared, and prepare your spouse, with some frank talk about finances.

YOUR KIDS

"Yippie," your kids will say. "Now Mom or Dad is at home all day." Before they consider you a new daytime playmate, sit down with your youngsters and explain what starting a business really means. First off: Err on the side of pessimism. Explain that while yes, you will be home all day, you'll be working and can't be disturbed. Let your kids know what your business is all about, whether it's writing textbooks or developing a new software program. Help them understand that you will be working all day long. Second, don't be afraid to talk finances. If starting your business means a financial sacrifice, explain to them that you may not be going to Walt Disney World this winter, or that trips to McDonald's will be fewer and farther between. Make them feel a part of the process and convey your enthusiasm for your work. Tell them exactly why you started the business. The more they understand, the less likely they will feel resentful that you're choosing to work alone in the spare bedroom instead of playing hide-and-seek in the backyard with them. This arrangement, you should remind them, will benefit all of you in the long run. You'll still be more available than you were when you commuted. But they must respect the boundaries you've set.

Repeat after us: Be patient. Educating your family and your friends takes time. Many work-at-home moms and dads recommend weekly family meetings. And one is never enough. Your five-year-old will have to be reminded what the DO NOT DISTURB sign means. And your eldest might not realize the stereo is too loud. So figure it will take six months or so for the new lifestyle to be accepted and understood by your kids and your spouse. At your weekly meetings you can tell your kids how your business is doing and listen to their gripes. This is a chance for your kids to see real work happening. "It's like Take Your Daughters to Work Day every day," laughs Ellen Parlapiano. And it often has the same enlightening effect. Her kids were so proud of their author mom, they announced to the bus driver that she had written a book.

SET LIMITS ON YOUR TIME AND SPACE

Nothing is a bigger credibility wrecker than announcing you cannot be disturbed all day and then plopping down in front of the U.S. Open for two hours. After you let your friends and family know your hours, stick to them. Jessica Schairer, a psychologist and expert on the trials of the self-employed, suggests you schedule time for your kids and spouse. Make it a point to let your family know when you will be eating dinner with them or when you will be taking your kid to soccer practice. Mike Waters starts work at 4 A.M. on certain days so he can spend time with his daughter when she gets home from school. He tells her in advance that he'll be around so they can work on school projects or goof off together.

Be clear with your instructions. If you say you cannot be disturbed except for emergencies, explain what you mean. For example, an emergency is not a quick ride to the mall or help rewinding the Barney video. It is an important phone call, the smell of leaking gas, or bleeding, bruises, or broken bones.

REMIND YOURSELF WHY YOU WANTED TO WORK AT HOME IN THE FIRST PLACE

Lest you forget, write down the reasons and post them someplace visible. If reason number one was to spend more time with your kids, then don't become a workaholic and shut them out. If it was to have more control over your time, don't let outsiders cramp your style, forcing you to pull all-nighters or work weekends. If another reason was to lead a less stressful life, then keep your business at a pace you can manage. And when work starts to overflow, consider hiring help or farming out projects to colleagues. If yet another reason was to pursue a passion, then stay focused on running the parts of the business that give you the most pleasure. Running your own business can be a potential burnout if you don't keep your priorities in front of you. Twelve-hour days won't drive you nuts if you want to make a million dollars, but they will wear you down if your aim was to decompress from the corporate treadmill. Remember, this is your ship. Be vigilant about staying out of tributaries that will pull you off course.

FOR MORE INFORMATION

• *Mompreneurs* by Ellen H. Parlapiano and Patricia Cobe ($13.00; Pedigree).
• *Honey, I Want to Start My Own Business* by Azriela Jaffe ($23.00; HarperBusiness).
• *Making It on Your Own* by Paul and Sarah Edwards ($12.00; Jeremy P. Tarcher/Putnam).

• *Entrepreneurial Couples Success Letter* (azjaffe@aol.com), a free bimonthly E-mail newsletter for working couples.

• Entrepreneurial Mothers Association, nonprofit run by moms who own their own businesses (602-892-0722).

• Home-Based Working Moms (HBWM), an organization for working women. Benefits include a monthly newsletter and a Web site where members can advertise their businesses. Dues are $34/year. For information send a SASE to HBWM PO Box 500164, Austin, TX 78750, call 512-918-0670 or visit their Web site (http://www.hbwm.com).

CHAPTER 8

Growing Your Company

Congratulations! You're finally on solid ground. Cash flow is positive, your product is a success—you're even sleeping through the night. But if you're like most entrepreneurs, you're itching to make another move. Perhaps you've discovered a promising new product, or you feel ready to target a larger audience. One problem: You're reluctant to jeopardize your hard-won security.

True, growing your business requires taking on risk. But the good news is that you're no longer a neophyte. You know what it takes to be successful in a hypercompetitive marketplace. And you've proven yourself already. Lenders who looked at you as a home business hack the first time around will now see you as a serious entrepreneur. That means you're far more likely to obtain the funding you need to take your business to new heights.

But don't expect to fly solo anymore. At the very least you'll have to bring in temps to handle more work or hire a full-time employee. In other words, the nature of your business will change. We'll help ease the growing pains by showing the best ways to:

- Identify new markets
- Hire the help you need
- Find more cash
- Create more office space

Keep an Eye on New Opportunities

You probably launched your company to fill a need in society that you spotted. To make the business grow, however, you must be on the lookout for new needs, or find more customers who want the product or service you offer. But such moves can be riddled with difficulties. To get started on the right foot, make sure you have an updated plan to guide you. As you grow, you'll discover that it's more important to be systematic. What's more, by revising your business and marketing plans, you'll stay focused on your goals—and keep within your budget.

Consider setting up an advisory board, too. Everyone needs to bounce ideas off of a smart, unbiased source. If you can't afford a paid board of directors, start an informal board by enlisting friends and family members. Try to include a lawyer, a CPA, a marketing specialist, and a business consultant if you can. They'll help guide you as you expand your business in the following ways:

ADD NEW SERVICES OR PRODUCTS

We won't kid around—introducing a new product requires up-front dollars, further research, testing, and eventually more promotions. Even if you set up a perfect launch, you're not assured of a slam dunk. Competitors may overtake you, or you may stumble. Taking on new responsibilities is rarely easy.

This time around, however, you're not starting from ground zero. You've introduced a product or service into the market at least once already, and you're more familiar with your customers' likes and dislikes. You've had time to observe their habits and spending tendencies, and your intuition is more highly developed. So trust your gut. If you think you've pinpointed a profitable gap in the market, by all means try to fill it. But don't neglect to involve your customers in the process of developing your idea. Let a number of them try out your new product or service before you turn on the factory wheels full blast.

Keep in mind, too, that you'll lower your risk by rolling out a product or service similar to one you already deliver. Financial planners, for instance, may want to become CPAs so that they can handle their clients' taxes, in addition to their investment portfolios. A management consultant may branch out from giving advice on restructuring to providing product feasibility analysis. A PR specialist could start writing annual reports, as well as brochures and press releases.

Bringing out a new product typically requires a larger investment than adding a service, so tread extra carefully. Your best bet, again, is to go with a related product. For instance, when Carmela Cantisani's French salad dressing began to sell well, she realized that there was increasing demand for gourmet food. "People were becoming more conscious of good food, not just health food," she says. "They still wanted food that was healthy but they wanted it to taste good." So she increased her line of salad dressings and added a balsamic vinaigrette made with Italian herbs and a low-fat "Provençal" dressing made with purée of white beans instead of oil. "I'd like to go into other products," she says, "but I realize I should wait until my salad dressing line is more established."

Another way to grow is to take a product you already have and find new uses for it. Cory Johnson started his business, Container Alternatives, to provide gardeners with a composite powder mix for creating planters and other outdoor garden products. Later, he realized that there was also a market for the finished product. So he spun off another business called Village Stoneman, which sells a series of already molded containers to garden enthusiasts.

You may even have the opportunity to take over another company's product line. Home-based entrepreneur Phil Smith, for instance, is particularly well positioned for making careful, informed acquisitions. As president of One World Projects, a company that distributes and sells sustainable rainforest products, Smith gets a bird's-eye view on what sells well. Then, if the opportunity arises, he'll buy the company whose product he merely used to distribute. "Since these companies have been my suppliers," he says, "I already know the product and how well it does." He recently acquired a company that imports animal carvings and jewelry from Ecuador made from the ivorylike tagua nut. "A lot of companies that sell rainforest products were started by people with strong ethics but maybe not a strong business sense," he says. By the time they come to Smith, they often just want someone to buy the inventory and take on the business at no extra cost.

MOVE INTO NEW MARKETS

Opportunity doesn't have to come in the form of new goods and services. In fact, many entrepreneurs do better shedding less profitable products and focusing on core strengths. "We offer fewer services than we did in the past, but we provide greater depth," says Larry Dressler of the home-based consulting practice Creative Team Solutions. At one time, Dressler and his partner got involved in doing business feasibility studies and restructuring reports for clients, in addition to team building. But their real strength was in helping companies create effective teams. "Now we have 12 approaches to team development and 20 topics on training, where we used to have only six," says Dressler. "Over time, we simply discovered that this is where our competency was."

Besides streamlining your offerings, consider introducing them in new markets. After all, products that catch on like wildfire in one industry will often ignite just as quickly in another, related industry. Take, for instance, the software product EIDA (which stands for the cryptic Extensible Interface Developer for Applications). Created by Igenesis, a software development and consulting company, EIDA helps computer users navigate databases and mine information with greater ease. Customers as diverse as Wall Street trading firms and technology product companies use EIDA. "Next we may place it in industries like insurance and health," says Srinivasan Sriram, who runs Igenesis out of the basement of his home.

Don't overlook expanding your business by tapping new distribution channels, too. Department stores, other retail chains, or mail-order catalogs like Lillian Vernon might prove to be good outlets for your product. Start by sending a package with promotional material and a product sample, and then follow up with a phone call. If the outlet you selected thinks your product will sell, it will buy a small sample to test. Carmela Cantisani, for instance, periodically sends her salad dressing to places like Williams-Sonoma. So far, she hasn't sparked the company's interest, but she plans to keep sending samples. Who knows, next year a buyer may be looking for a product like hers to add to its mix.

If you offer a specialized service, you could market it to customers around the country via carefully placed ads in trade publications or business journals. You may even consider opening a satellite office in a favorite vacation destination. Financial planner D. J. Shah, for instance, is investigating the possibility of opening a branch office in Salt Lake City. While continuing his home-based practice in the Boston area, he would spend one week a month in Utah, most likely basing his practice in a rented condominium. He chose Salt Lake City because it boasts a growing community and is home to his mentor. What's more, says Shah, "There's great fishing and skiing out there!"

FOR MORE INFORMATION

• Subscribe to specialized business magazines covering your industry, and keep tabs on how other businesses are growing by reading *Inc.* ($19; 800-234-0999), *Your Company* (free to American Express corporate card holders, $4 an issue for non–card holders; 800-528-2122), and *Entrepreneur* ($19.97; 800-274-6229).

Get the Help You Need

Entrepreneurs are an independent lot. They have a vision, and they're determined to carry it out single-handedly. But you can't do everything from filing papers to finding new customers, especially when business starts to build. How do you know when you need help? If you tend to ignore the subtle signs—like the darkening rings under your eyes and last month's three-digit coffee bill—you should periodically try this exercise: List all the activities you need to do to run your business optimally (Note: This list may include a lot of tasks that get short shrift!). Next, indicate how much time you *should* devote to each responsibility. If the time needed to operate your business exceeds what you can manage (and still have a life), face it, you need help.

But what tasks should you farm out? Savvy entrepreneurs start by passing on the mundane-but-necessary parts of business so that they can spend more time on sales and other activities that generate revenue. For instance, you may need a clerk to do your filing, help fill orders, or assist with a direct-mail campaign. If you've been doing your own bookkeeping or preparing your taxes, get help with these areas.

Before hiring someone to work out of your office, however, check into local zoning laws. Many areas forbid home entrepreneurs from having employees. If you run into a snag, apply for a variance (refer to Chapter 1 for a refresher). Once you've squared away that issue, you can get started. Most likely you'll need to bundle jobs together. If you brought on both a secretary and a purchasing clerk, for instance, you might not have enough work to keep them busy. But you can fold the two positions together and create sufficient work for one.

Whatever the job is, define what you expect from your employee—and put it in writing. A job description gets you and the worker on the same page. If you're leery about taking someone on full time, test that person out on a part-time basis. You may find that you only need an assistant half the day, and many people prefer part-time work. Parents with young children, for instance, sometimes don't want to work an eight-hour day. Retirees also look for part-time work, and they offer years of experience, as well as greater stability than younger workers.

When you start hiring—even if you only take on one person—you become a manager. It's unavoidable. And it isn't easy. "The amount of effort and skill it took to manage a staff was a surprise to me," says Sriram, who has six full-time employees in the United States and 35 in India. When he first started running into problems with his staff, Sriram turned to other businesspeople to see if they had similar problems. "Talking to other small business owners gave me some insights," he says. Fortunately, he also discovered that he has a natural knack for motivating people. As you start to hire employees, don't be shy about seeking advice. Like Sriram, you may learn by doing—and by talking to experienced managers. If you need further guidance, consider taking a management training course to help you learn to draw the best from your employees.

USE SUBCONTRACTORS

As you'll soon realize, hiring people is expensive. In addition to salaries, you have to pay half of your employee's FICA taxes

(7.65% of the first $65,400 in pay and 1.45% of everything thereafter in 1997). There are also federal and state unemployment taxes to consider, as well as workers' compensation taxes. The amount varies from state to state, so check with your accountant. And don't forget about the high cost of benefits like health insurance, annual paid vacation, and life insurance, if you offer them.

Rather than take on the cost and paperwork involved in hiring employees, you can delegate functions like data processing and marketing to subcontractors. An advantage to hiring a subcontractor is that you can hire extra help only when you have extra work. When business slows down again, you don't have the late-night worries of making payroll. For instance, when Larry Dressler gets a big assignment, he brings on other team-building consultants to help him. "For this kind of work, I can't imagine finding someone by placing an ad," he says. "Instead, I call my network and get personal referrals. Then I have a face-to-face interview, and I might actually put the candidate through a routine in which they have to do a training segment in front of a group of people."

One word of warning: Clients may prefer to work with you over a subcontractor. "In a service-based business, you are the company," says Millie Szerman, who runs a home-based marketing and public relations business specializing in the gift industry. "People want to deal with me, and unfortunately that limits me to some degree." Dressler worked around this problem by stressing his company's training techniques. "My partner and I were interested in some degree of growth and to do that, we had to market an approach, not just the services of two people," he explains. So his marketing materials don't emphasize the owners' skills. Instead, they call attention to a business philosophy.

To gauge your comfort level with a potential subcontractor, ask some basic questions: Has the person or firm worked with businesses like yours in the past? Does the subcontractor understand and agree with your way of doing business? You must also make sure he or she is familiar with rules laid down by regulatory agencies important to your market, such as the Federal Communications Commission or the Food and Drug Administration. And, of course, you need to determine whether or not the subcontractor will give your needs sufficient priority and meet the deadlines you impose.

Another tricky issue is assessing the subcontractor's intentions. You don't want to get burned by someone looking to acquire knowledge of your technology and eventually take over your clients. That's one reason to have a clear contract that outlines responsibilities and keeps decision making in your hands. Spell out what info is to be kept in the family—and the penalties for disclosing it. If you pay a subcontractor to design a software program or special equipment, for instance, be sure to retain full ownership rights. Don't neglect to get a copy of the IRS Publication 937, too, which outlines who is likely to be classified as an independent contractor or an employee. Your contract must comply with IRS guidelines. Otherwise, your subcontractor could be misclassified, possibly costing you thousands of dollars in back taxes and penalties. (For more information, see Chapter 4.)

CALL ON THE TEMP FORCE

This is also a great way to fill a slot when business booms. Temps can help you with mailings or filling large orders. There are even professional temps—like lawyers and CPAs. A bonus to hiring a temp is that someone else does the screening for you. What's more, the agency handles the paperwork that you would have to do if you were employing the worker directly. Of course, you may pay as much as 50% more for the convenience.

If you need longer-term employees—or even a full staff—turn to so-called staff-leasing companies. Similar to temp agencies, they will interview and hire employees for you and pay their salaries. You dump the paperwork, and your crew gains much better benefits than you could offer. That's because staff-leasing companies typically have thousands of employees and can therefore purchase health coverage, life insurance, and other perks at lower, pooled rates.

HIRE A FAMILY MEMBER

When most soloists need help, they look no farther than the room next door where their teenager is engrossed in "Beverly Hills 90210." In fact, family members are a top employment source, says Carolyn Tice, executive editor of *Home Business News*, a quarterly magazine of the American Home Business Association. What's more, hiring your child saves on income tax. Let's say your child's earnings exceeded the standard deduction of $4,000 in 1997. The excess would be taxed at the child's lower rate of 15% for federal taxes. But let's say that the child earned $6,000. If he or she invested $2,000 in an Individual Retirement Account, the smart kid would dodge taxes altogether. What's more, you don't have to pay Social Security taxes on wages you pay your child, as long as he or she is under age 18.

Hiring your children also teaches them about your business—and gives them a solid work ethic. But don't give them tasks that are out of their range—or too menial. You don't want to bore them to tears stuffing envelopes every day. Treat them like any other employee by gradually giving them more and more responsibility—and reward them in kind.

PICK A PARTNER

How many times have you wished that there was another one of you? Instead of wishing for a duplicate, however, you should try to find someone who complements you. Of course, that's no simple task. Usually partners develop a business together, gradually learning each other's strengths and weaknesses. But if you've been going it solo and now want a mate, don't worry—your professional contacts and friends can help you find a good one. Flip through your Rolodex and you may even be able to put together a list of candidates right now. After all, as your business has developed, you've met many people through professional associations, trade shows, conventions, and other industry events.

Of course, choosing a partner requires far more consideration and soul-searching than hiring an employee. A partner shares in business liabilities—and therefore also takes part in decision making. That makes it especially important to find someone you respect. When you meet with potential partners, try to determine if they share your vision. If the partner is your spouse, you'll also need to discuss how not to let business pervade your non-work life. Once you feel comfortable with a possible partner, go over the nitty-gritty, including:

• **How to split responsibilities.** To avoid confusion and miscommunication, you should divide up different parts of the business, taking care to draw on your areas of expertise.

• **How you'll share profits.** You've already invested a lot of savings and hard work in your business. So unless your partner is bringing his or her own clients and equipment to the table, you probably won't divide profits evenly. For instance, you may agree on an arrangement in which the new partner gradually buys shares in the company. No matter how you decide to structure the deal, get everything in writing.

• **How you'll handle problems.** Even if your partner is your best friend, you need to plan for the worst. If the relationship sours—and it could—you must have a buyout plan in place. Or what if you want to retire earlier than your partner? If one of you is in a car accident, you may need a succession plan. No matter how optimistic you are about the future, you must discuss these possibilities—and outline how you'll handle them in a contract.

FOR MORE INFORMATION

• *Managing for Dummies*, by Bob Nelson and Peter Economy, gives former soloists excellent tips on how to draw the most from employees ($19.99; IDG Books Worldwide).
• Dale Carnegie offers leadership and management training classes (212-921-4315 for locations nearest you).

Financing Your Expansion

Now for the fun part: finding the money to fund your ambitious plan. A good place to start is back at the beginning. Remember that cash flow statement you drafted? Ooh, when was it—back when your office was on the kitchen table and your biggest challenge was finding a few grand for a new PC and a fax machine? Well, time to dust off that relic and start anew (see page 64 in Chapter 3 for a sample cash flow statement). You need to figure out how much your expansion will cost, when you will need the money, and for how long. When David Bruno wanted to boost sales of his inspirational card collection he found he needed extra cash around Christmas to pay suppliers. So he secured a $30,000 line of credit from his bank. Smart move. A line of credit makes sense for seasonal or short-term cash flow droughts. With a line you draw down cash when you need it and then pay it back when business picks up. Typically you can open up a line for $25,000 to as much as $500,000. You must, of course, renew the line each year. Bruno could pay off his debt quickly in January, when his customers paid up.

Once you have a handle on your capital needs, then you can figure out what type of financing makes the most sense. If, like Bruno, you just need cash to pay bills during slow times, then a line of credit is best. But if you need $1 million to buy a manufacturing plant or develop a new software product, and you don't have sufficient collateral to secure a bank loan, then you'll have to seek other financing sources, like venture capital or angel investors.

Before you start knocking on your banker's door or seeking angels on the Internet, tap your network for advice. Your board of advisors is the logical place to start. Also, pick the brains of entrepreneurial colleagues who are moving on the fast track. If you don't have such pals, search for them by attending chamber of commerce meetings, chatting up other business owners on the Internet, going to business seminars, and joining organizations where you meet like-minded folks, like the Center for Entrepreneurial Management (212-925-7304).

Pump your newfound friends for information on how they financed *their* expansion. Was it a bank loan, an angel investment, or a wealthy customer? Ask for references to bankers, accountants, and other lending sources. "You need personal contacts to get access to capital, otherwise you are at the bottom of the pile," says Joe Mancuso, small business guru and author of numerous books, including *Mancuso's Small Business Basics*.

Bernice Mast learned about the Manhattan Borough Development Corporation's (MBDC) loan program when she attended a Microsoft small business seminar. The director of the program was giving a talk on business plans. Mast introduced herself after the class and asked how she could qualify for a loan. Eventually Mast applied for and was given a $20,000 three-year equipment loan from MBDC. Up until then, she had financed her expansion through credit cards. "Getting the loan gave me an extra level of seriousness about the shape of my business," says Mast.

Another source of financing expertise, says Mancuso: your accountant, particularly if he or she is plugged into the small business world. Such an expert will know bankers and venture capitalists and be familiar with government lending programs. If your present accountant is not a small business whiz, shop for one who is.

True, networking is an excellent way to find money, but you have to know the financing ropes. Here are some strategies that you can use to make your business grow. We've listed them in order of small to large borrowing needs:

CUSTOMERS

To keep cash flowing, offer your customers a 5% discount if they pay up front. Or suggest that if they pay upon completion of your work—rather than after the standard 30-day payment period—you will give them a 2% discount. This method will get cash in your till faster and will give your customers a break at the same time.

BANK FINANCING

To qualify for a bank loan, you'll need to have solid financials: Your cash flow must be strong enough to support loan payments, your credit history must be sound, and you must have collateral in case your business fails before the loan is paid off. If you don't have the bricks and mortar that banks want but need capital to fuel your growth, skip down to the section on private placements. Also review financing sources listed in Chapter 3, such as Small Business Administration (SBA) guaranteed loans.

That said, don't let glitches in your finances completely deter you from trying to get bank financing. Bruno had a marred credit history (he'd declared personal bankruptcy in June 1987) and knew obtaining bank loans would be tricky. But once his business became profitable he brought his banker his business plan and sales report. Bruno explained his business concept and vowed he'd be back when he was ready to make a move. A year later, when earnings were soaring and he wanted to add a new product line, Bruno went back to his banker, who said, "Yes, you are ready for a loan." In addition to his line of credit he was granted a $15,000 term loan. A term loan allows you to take out a big chunk of change and then pay it back in three to five years. A final word about bank loans: Watch for special low-rate loan deals from your bank, or ask your banker when the next one is planned. Lenders will periodically offer loans at the prime rate to lure new customers.

PRIVATE PLACEMENTS

When you need big bucks but your business is too risky for a bank loan, you can raise cash on your own by selling shares of your company. Though you lose some control—venture capitalists often take a seat on your board and will undoubtedly meddle in the daily affairs of your business—the bright side is that you're not saddled with hefty loan payments. What's more, angels or venture capitalists typically will provide expert advice and guidance on everything from marketing to financing to manufacturing.

Venture capital. If you're well on your way to the big leagues with the Microsofts and America Onlines and need megabucks to get there, venture capital may be your best bet. Venture capitalists typically fund high-tech, hot-growth firms with revenues of over $10 million. A venture capitalist rarely invests less than $1 million—the average is around $5 million. To qualify for such lofty sums, you must prove you're on a winning trajectory. Venture capitalists want to make five times their money in five years, says Mancuso. The best way to find a venture capitalist is through your network of colleagues. Also go to the library and browse through *Pratt's Guide to Venture Capital Sources*. This tome lists 1,175 venture capitalists, the projects they invest in, how much they invest, and what area of the country they work in. The National Venture Capital Association (703-351-5269) also has a comprehensive directory of its 230 members.

Angels. Sounds ideal, right? A beneficent benefactor who will swoop down and bestow thousands of dollars on your

189

growing business. Well, not quite. Angels are savvy investors who look for fast-growing firms that will give them a greater return on their money than traditional investments. There are about 250,000 angels across the country who invest $10 to $20 billion annually in nearly 40,000 small businesses, according to the Center for Venture Research at the University of New Hampshire. To qualify you must be able to promise a growth rate of about 15% a year and a 20% return on initial investments. Angels may invest individually or in groups and typically invest $10,000 to $500,000 per business. How do you find an angel? Most angels invest in companies within a half-day's travel from their home or office, so personal and local contacts are best. There are also a dozen or so angel networks, including the SBA's Angel Capital Electronic Network (ACE-Net), an Internet service, started in 1996. ACE-Net links angels with small, innovative companies who need $250,000 to $5 million (http://ace-net.unh.edu). Angels can search the database for companies by such criteria as industry, size, and age.

Small Business Investment Companies (SBICs). Need money but can't promise get-rich-quick profits? Try approaching an SBIC. These private-venture capital firms receive part of their funding from the SBA. The SBA created SBICs in the '50s to help cash-hungry start-ups that would not qualify for traditional venture capital financing. SBICs differ from regular venture capital firms in a number of ways: (1) They lend smaller amounts, $495,000 is the average, compared to a minimum of $1 million for most venture capital deals; (2) they fund smaller companies. In fact, 20% of an SBICs investments must be in companies with earnings under $2 million and net worths of no more than $6 million; (3) they're more lenient. SBICs, for instance, may allow you to use equipment as collateral and typically don't require a large equity position in your firm. As with all venture capital or angel deals, each SBIC focuses on specifc industries like manufacturing or technology—so approach one whose goals jibe with yours. The SBA's *SBIC Directory* (202-205-7589) will help you narrow your search. You can also download SBIC listings from the SBA Web site at http://www.sba.gov.

Private offerings. If you can't attract venture capital or an angel investor, another alternative is a private offering. In such a transaction, you solicit smaller investments from a group of individuals. The advantages are that you may be able to raise more cash and give up a smaller stake in your company. You decide how much equity you want to give up (venture capitalists, for instance, usually want a 40% to 60% stake). The disadvantage is that a private offering can be time consuming and costly. What's more, following the offering you'll have to maintain communications with many investors, rather than just one if you'd gone the venture capital route. For more information, the SEC's Web site (http://www.sec.gov.smbus1.htm) provides information and guidelines on private and public stock offerings.

FOR MORE INFORMATION

• The SBA publishes a number of useful pamphlets on how to run your business (800-827-5722) including *Financial Management for the Growing Business*, EB-7; *Financing for the Small Business*, FM-14.

• Center for Entrepreneurial Management (CEM), 180 Varick Street, New York, NY 10014; 212-633-0060. The $96 membership fee includes a free subscription to *Inc.* and *Success* magazines, as well CEM's own monthly newsletter.

• *How to Start, Finance and Manage Your Own Small Business* by Joseph R. Mancuso ($17.00, Simon & Schuster; you can order from CEM: 212-633-0060).

• *Pratt's Guide to Venture Capital Sources* (Venture Economics).

• *Directory of Venture Capital* by Catherine E. Lister and Thomas D. Harnish ($34.95, John Wiley & Sons; 800-225-5945).

Creating More Office Space

The downside to pumping up your product line or adding new employees: You might have to move. But that doesn't necessarily mean you have to move out of the house. You probably started your business at home for good reasons: to keep your overhead low, to be near your kids, or to avoid those nasty rush-hour commutes. Do you have to give all this up in order to let your business grow? Not necessarily. True, moving out may enhance your credibility and give you extra room for your new staff and to entertain clients. But you can also find ways to expand and still keep your business at home. At this point you have to decide what your priorities are and then explore the possibilities. Even though his business was growing and many of his clients lived in Manhattan, Steve Bromberger, a CPA in Plainsboro, New Jersey, decided staying at home was paramount. So he added an extra room to his house and now rents an office in Manhattan for three months during the busy tax season. However, when work treads on your private life, then you may need to take your business elsewhere. Ken Godat and Jeff Jonczyk, who run a graphic design business from their home in Tucson, Arizona, knew the time had come when they found themselves taking turns feeding paper into their laser printer late one night while watching a ("gripping") Joan Crawford movie.

STAYING HOME

If there's no place like home, then think creatively. Like Bromberger, you can add on. Or you can take over another room in your house or buy a bigger home to accommodate family *and* business.

Work with what you have. Is there a spare room you can appropriate? Can you move the business to the garage or relocate to your finished basement? Jeff Wuorio, a freelance writer, decided he'd rather convert his maintenance shed into an office than fight rush-hour traffic to get to work. If you're being edged out by boxes of product samples and a few years' worth of old business records, move it all to a rental storage space. If your problem is finding space to meet with clients, look for off-site locations. Tom Roncelli, a real estate broker, conducts business meetings over breakfast at a local restaurant. For larger gatherings, he asks his bank to loan him a room for an hour or two. Roncelli says vendors or clients are often willing to lend their own conference facilities: It brings new consumers into their domain and for you it solidifies the business relationship.

Build an addition. If there's no more space at home, don't despair—call a builder. Bromberger, faced with a $2,000 monthly rent tab for office space in Manhattan, decided it was more cost effective to put on a $30,000, 24-by-16 addition. What's more, Bromberger says, he has increased the value of his home. But before you hire a contractor, make sure your zoning laws allow home office additions. A quick phone call to the local planning board will give you an answer (see Chapter 1).

Buy a new home. If you're landlocked from expansion, consider moving to a new home. Michael Hoffman, a public relations consultant, had "mentally and physically" outgrown his office, but his 900-square-foot condo in Laguna Niguel, California, had no space to give. Hoffman, who says he is most productive working at home, decided to trade up. Now he owns a three-bedroom 2,250-square-foot house in nearby Dana Point. Says Hoffman, "It's very inviting for clients to visit me in my home office. It builds a closer relationship."

MOVING OUT

Our advice when moving to your first "real office": Don't take on more space or more rent than you can afford. You can start small and still have room to grow by, say, sharing space or services with other businesses.

If you're not quite ready to fly solo, consider a **business incubator.** These are commercial spaces, run by nonprofit groups, that help nurture small companies. There are over 500 incubators across the country that provide office space and support services for small start-ups. An incubator is an excellent starting ground, especially if you need support staff like a receptionist and equipment like copy machines, faxes, and computers. What's more, incubators typically have experts on staff who can help hone your business or marketing plans. And because you are housed with fellow entrepreneurs you have a built-in network to swap ideas and financing tips. Getting in can be competitive. You must have a solid business concept (not necessarily written) that proves you've carefully thought out your business's future. Call or write to the National Business Incubation Association for more information (20 East Circle Drive, Suite 190, Athens, OH 45701; 614-593-4331) or log onto their Web site (http://www.nbia.org).

If you're not quite ready to go whole hog on a new office but need support services, an **executive suite** may be the ideal solution. These are run by for-profit enterprises and offer myriad upscale services. Pay one monthly fee and you can get a furnished office complete with a receptionist to take your phone messages and greet clients, a meeting room, and a kitchen. Some suites offer other boons like travel services and videoconferencing. Before you sign a lease, ask what you get for your monthly rent. Many start nickel-and-diming you for extras like copies and faxes and kitchen use—services you might have assumed would be free. For a list of executive suite locations in your area call the Executive Suite Association (800-237-4741).

If you want autonomy but can't find affordable solo space,

then consider **shared space.** This can be an ideal arrangement. You'll get relatively low rent, without the burden of a commercial lease. David Spivey, an employee trainer, subleases a single 400-square-foot office in an 8,000-square-foot building in Dallas. Three businesses leased the entire building (one of which was owned by a friend) but found they only needed 70% of the space. Spivey stepped in to fill the void. Included in his $400 rent is use of a common reception area, kitchen, and bathroom. You can also rent space with a colleague. Just remember that if you both sign the lease, you are both obligated for the rent for the full term. If your relationship sours, you could end up in a sticky legal battle.

If you want to have total control over your environment, then **rent alone.** Like most home-based entrepreneurs, Gregg Winter, a New York City mortgage broker, was used to having it his way. He also needed a place big enough to accommodate his growing business and five employees. So when he decided to leave his brownstone in Brooklyn for a real office in Manhattan, he looked for a space of his own. But Winter also wanted to minimize his risk. He opted for a 1,500-square-foot space in a small office building that only required a fresh coat of paint, and leased it for just two years.

CHOOSE THE RIGHT OFFICE

This is new territory—picking out the best office for your needs. First, a few words of warning. Don't be seduced by the window dressing. A marble lobby with busts of Greek gods or a sun-filled space with a view might be nice. But make sure they're taking out the trash and that the security system works. Ask tough questions. If you want a pro to help you, hire an experienced realtor. Whether you go it alone or hire a pro, you need to consider some specific issues before starting your search. Finally, before you sign a lease, make sure your lawyer reviews the contract.

1. Location. Where do you need to be: Near a FedEx office? A top-notch printer? The train station to make your commute less onerous? If clients will be visiting, how accessible is the office? Is there sufficient parking? How's traffic? Is the area noisy? Winter had his heart set on an office in trendy Soho. But when he visited the space in the afternoon, he found the 5 P.M. traffic, with honking horns and screeching brakes, an unbearable obstacle. He settled for a quieter space with thicker windows uptown.

2. Ambience. Coming from a home office, you'll want your new digs to feel, well, homey. Comfort, however, is a matter of personal taste. Are the ceilings too low or too high? Are those fluorescent lights too harsh? Is the color scheme in the building drab or too glitzy? Is the lobby a place that shines with professionalism? Winter answered a number of these questions when he left his sunny brownstone. For him it was important to have lots of sunlight (he'd had a terrace back home), wall space to hang artwork, and of course a semblance of peace and quiet to concentrate on his deals.

4. Amenities. Will the building meet your needs? If you work late, will there be adequate security? Is the heat sufficient? Does the space have enough electrical outlets, phone jacks, and elbow room? Is there a concierge or doorman to take in packages or greet clients? Are there meeting rooms you can use, and do you have access on holidays? How well is the building maintained? Ask, for instance, how often the floors are cleaned, the garbage removed, and the windows washed.

5. Neighbors. Check out the businesses on your floor. If you have clients visiting you may not want them to walk past a high-traffic office like a residential rental agency or a photo processing lab (the fumes can make you sick). Ask about the building's turnover rate. A high turnover rate, when offices change hands every two years, may indicate that the building is poorly managed or that it attracts fly-by-night businesses. If you are a professional, like a lawyer or therapist, consider space near fellow colleagues for credibility. Finally, knock on the doors of your would-be neighbors to find out what kind of people you'll be passing in the hall each day. Once you leave home, they'll be like family.

FOR MORE INFORMATION

• *Leasing Office Space You Can Afford* by Robert J. Cook ($29.95, Probus; 800-634-3966).

• *Commercial Tenant's Leasing Transactions Guide* by Alan D. Sugarman and Joel J. Goldberg ($135, John Wiley & Sons; 800-225-5945).

BEST HOME BUSINESS RESOURCES

Associations

American Home Business Association (HBA): Offers training and support programs, as well as benefits, including a discount telephone service, unsecured credit line of up to $100,000, health insurance, discount pharmacy, term life insurance, disability insurance, and help with setting up IRAs, 401(k) plans, and SEPs. Publishes the quarterly magazine *Home Business News*, a monthly newsletter, and provides members with a subscription to *Home Office Computing*. (Membership cost: $39 enrollment fee and $30 fee every three months; 800-758-8500; http://www.homebusiness.com).

National Association for the Self-Employed (NASE): With a full-time advocacy staff, NASE has the strongest voice on Capitol Hill. It also offers more than 100 benefits to its members, including educational materials, scholarships, discounted telephone service, travel rebates, a toll-free business-consultant service, and a health plan. With 320,000 members, it's the largest association of small business owners. (Membership: $72 a year; 800-232-NASE; http:www.nase.org).

SOHO America/Small Office Home Office (SOHO): Gives small entrepreneurs a voice in Washington, D.C. Offers a fax-on-demand library with articles about building and running a business, and it sends a weekly electronic newsletter. Provides discounts on office products, printing, magazine subscriptions, long-distance telephone service, and travel. (Membership: $33 a year; 800-495-SOHO; info@soho.org).

Books

Getting Business to Come to You, by home business gurus Paul and Sarah Edwards and Laura Clampitt Douglas, is an excellent guide to direct marketing, advertising, and publicity ($11.95; Jeremy P. Tarcher/Putnam).

Guerilla Marketing: Secrets for Making Big Profits from Your Small Business is Jay Conrad Levinson's blueprint for finding customers and keeping them ($12.95; Houghton Mifflin Company).

How to Protect and Benefit From Your Ideas, a booklet published by the American Intellectual Property Law Association, offers information on patents and trademarks. Plus, you get a half-hour consultation with a member lawyer ($10; American Intellectual Property Law Association; 2001 Jefferson Davis Hwy., Suite 203; Arlington, Va. 22202-3694).

Selling for Dummies, by Tom Hopkins, gives practical and effective techniques for even the most tongue-tied salesperson ($16.99; IDG Books Worldwide).

Tax Savvy for Small Business, by tax attorney Frederick Daily, provides detailed information on business forms, including sole proprietorships and corporations ($26.95; Nolo Press).

The MONEY Book of Personal Finance by Richard Eisenberg is a good reference to turn to when you set up your health and retirement benefit plans ($24.95; Warner Books).

Government

Federal Trade Commission: Call the Public Reference Branch and order two sets of policy papers: *Advertising Policy on Ad Substantiation* and *Advertising Policy on Deception* (free; 202-326-2222).

Internal Revenue Service Publications: IRS Publication 334, *Tax Guide for Small Business*; 505, *Withholding and Estimated Taxes*; 587, *Business Use of Your Home*; 535, *Business Expenses*; 463, *Travel, Entertainment and Gift Expenses*; and 917, *Business Use of a Car* (free; 800-829-3676).

Small Business Administration (SBA): In addition to their lending programs, the SBA offers a wealth of free (and some not-so-free) publications. Write for a copy of the *Directory of Business Development Publications* (SBA Publications, PO Box 1000, Fort Worth, TX 76119). For information on guaranteed loans or other SBA programs, call the Small Business Answer Desk (800-827-5722) or log onto the SBA Web site (http://www.sba.gov).

U.S. Patent and Trademark Office: To protect you business, ask for the free booklets *Basic Facts about Registering a Trademark* and *Basic Facts about Patents* (800-PTO-9199).

Magazines

Home Office Computing, published by Scholastic, Inc., is an indispensable resource chock full of the latest news on home office technology, marketing tips, and business ideas ($19.97; 800-288-7812).

Inc., published by Goldhirsh Group 18 times a year, is geared to small-to-midsized companies. Articles cover strategic planning, management, and payment and profit sharing plans ($19; 800-234-0999).

Your Company, published six times a year by Time Inc. and American Express Publishing Corp., is jam-packed with creative marketing ideas, management techniques, technology updates, and more (free to corporate card holders, $4 an issue for non–card holders; 800-528-2122).

On-Line Support

American Demographics magazine will make you subscribe to get full services, but you can still tap a wealth of free information at its Web site (http://www.marketingtools.com).

AT&T's BUSINESS NETWORK includes an index of 1,000 Web sites for business users (http://www.att.com/bnet).

GO HOMEBUSINESS on CompuServe: A national forum sponsored by HBA, this is a great place to make contacts, share ideas, and participate in on-line conferences.

Guerilla Marketing's Web site offers a bonanza of marketing advice. Plus, you can subscribe to a free weekly E-mail newsletter (http://www.gmarketing.com).

Idea Cafe: Run by syndicated columnist Rhonda Abrams, this site offers periodic conferences with special guests like

"Dilbert" creator Scott Adams. You can pick up ideas and share your own in the "CyberSchmooz" café, too (http://www.ideacafe.com).

Open Market's Commercial Sites Index (http://www.directory.net), **BizWeb** (http://www.bizweb.com), **Big Book** (http://www.bigbook.com), and **Big Yellow** (http://www.bigyellow.com) are all sites that help you find information about companies, including your competitors.

Your Business on America Online gives a wealth of information for small businesses. You'll find a message board for home business owners, a legal resource area, and a finance center where you can download software.

Working from Home Forum on CompuServe (GO WORK) offers bulletin boards where you can post questions, a library with information on specific businesses such as desktop publishing and on general topics like accounting and taxes.

INDEX

INDEX